FROM ADDICTION TO FITNESS

Completing Ironmans to Self-Discovery on the Appalachian Trail

LOUIS M. CORMIER

ISBN: 978-1-912149-35-3

Map on page 4 courtesy of United States. National Park Service. Appalachian Trail Project Office; Cartography, Inc

To my wife who is the most patient
and loving person I know.

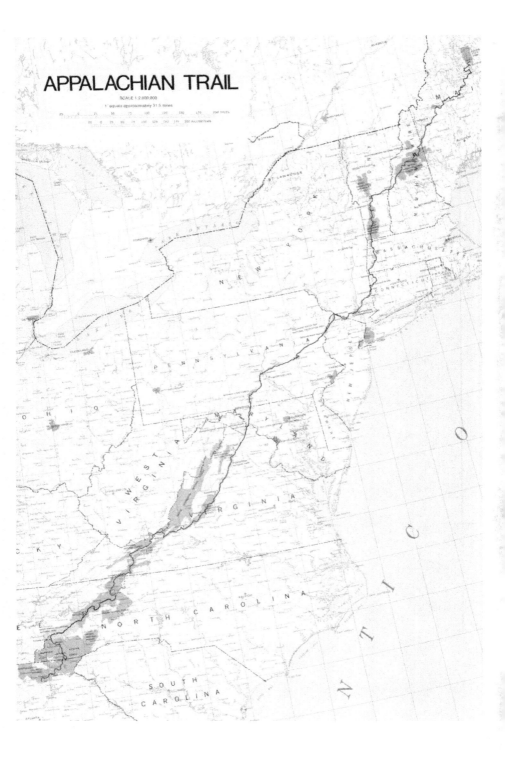

APPALACHIAN TRAIL

SCALE 1:2,000,000

1" equals approximately 31.5 miles

Contents

Preface 6

The Dark Hole 9

Detox 19

Sober 27

Retired.. 37

Katahdin 49

The Preparation.. 57

With Nat... 64

Finally on My Own 71

The Smokies... 79

Virginia... 87

Shenandoah.. 95

Harpers Ferry.. 104

PA... 112

Reflecting Back... 120

New York.. 128

Massachusetts – Vermont.. 139

New Hampshire 149

The Whites 160

Maine.. 169

The Last Week.. 176

About The Author... 185

Preface

Every time I told somebody a small part of my story they always said "You should write a book." However I did not want to write because I did not want to tell the whole story to my friends. I was always hiding from the truth. I did not want to be exposed for the rest of my life.

I come from a small village where most people know their neighbors. It's not like in the big cities. In small communities people like to gossip.

I figured I would write my story and publish it after I passed, that way I would not be exposed. My daughter Natalie kept encouraging me to write now because she knew I could help other people with addictions. It could motivate someone to get help.

In the end, I decided to write the story anyways, since all that happened is in the past. After hiking the Appalachian Trail, I have grown so much as a person. If I can help only one person with an addiction by telling my story, I feel it is worth telling. If I can help one person get off the couch and go out for a hike in the wilderness, they will grow inside, and it is worth telling my story.

This story is about a man who had to hit bottom before he realizes how much he had to lose. The hole was very deep and he had only two options, to fill the hole with dirt over himself or to climb out. The climb was very hard, but the reward outside the hole, with his feet back on level ground was so worth the effort.

Living a life with addiction is not easy. The only persons that can truly understand addiction is an addict. Looking passed an addiction is so hard, and the pain is so extreme. The worst part is the pain it does to friends and loved ones.

This man, me, has accomplished so much after overcoming the addiction. Things I never even dreamed of could become a reality. My life is so much better, but I will never be cured. Admitting that there is an addiction is the first step in recovery.

Avoiding the temptation is the next step. It's never over, but now that my addiction is under control my life is so wonderful. Life is so fragile but being healthy has so much more to offer than anything else.

So many people have helped me along the way, I cannot change the past, but the future has not been written yet. If I am exposed for telling the truth, so be it. Hopefully this will motivate someone.

I would like to thank you, Lucille, for all the support that you have given me since we got married over thirty-five years ago. We have four children together and raised them to be fine adults. I would also like to thank my children for the love that you gave me when the going got tough. Thank you very much.

Writing the book has open many wounds that had been pushed deep inside me. I had to dig very deep to go get some of it to come out. At the same time it has helped me heal those wounds. Hopefully, I can encourage somebody, somewhere and also help them heal.

Chapter 1

The Dark Hole

It was a cloudy and cold December afternoon when I got up. I had been drinking alone through the night. I knew today was going to be a very different day. I was forty-five years old and at the lowest and darkest point in my life. My wife, Lucille, had left the night before with our children, but I expected them to be back the next day when I got up. I scanned through the house, and it was quiet unlike other days; there were no sounds from the kids.

I looked everywhere for something to drink but could not find a single drop. I just hit bottom and had nowhere to go. Lucille had always had promised me no matter how bad things got she would never leave me. She had always stood by my side and loved me, but this time it was too much. I knew she would be at her mother's place, so I called her and asked her to come by and bring me something to drink and that I really needed to talk to her. It was too far to walk, and I had wrecked my vehicle a few days before, and had no way to get to the liquor store. I was feeling sick to my stomach still drunk and miserable and had no place to turn. To my surprise Lucille did come over, but she brought her younger brother along with her. I am not sure if she was afraid or maybe thought he could talk some sense into me, but it tore me up inside because that was the worst thing she could have done. I had no intention of ever hurting her physically. I loved her way too much to cause her any harm; however, the mental harm I was causing her was probably worse.

When I saw him, I could not think clearly anymore because he was the last person I wanted to see. I grabbed a knife out of the drawer. "You don't need to be here," I yelled. "This isn't your trouble. Now, get out!" I was not in great shape and still half-drunk, and he is bigger than me, so he easily took away the knife. I had no intention of hurting him. I did not even try to fight. Lucille told me to go to back to bed and she would be back later in the day and we could talk when I was sober later in that afternoon. I crawled back to bed, but when I got up, all my hunting guns, knives, lighters, pills and anything else I could hurt myself with was gone from the house. I had decided that I was going to end it, and Lucille had seen the signs and had taken precautions. That was also why she had taken the kids away.

So many thoughts were rushing through my head. I could not stand the thought of losing my family. I had contemplated committing suicide many times before but could not go through with it, knowing how much it would affect my children. I knew people who had committed suicide and saw how much it affected their family. I just could not let my family suffer for the rest of their lives because I was weak. They say there is always a light at the end of a dark tunnel, but that day I could not even see a small candle or glitter of hope. I was at a dead end in my life. I knew if I stopped drinking most of my problems would go away, however, I had tried so many times and had failed. I was in so much pain mentally. Extreme shame and guilt were rushing in my head.

I had wanted to quit drinking for quite some time. I knew if I did not quit Lucille would eventually leave me even though she kept saying she would never do it. Really who could blame her since I was not the same man she had married. My family was so important to me, and I desperately wanted and needed to quit for them, but I was possessed. I had promised her so many times I had drunk my last beer, or it was the last day I would drink. It was always the last something and then I would stop. I always had every intention of stopping, but when I tried, I would go through bad withdrawal. The only way I could stop feeling sick was to get a drink. I tried to ween myself off many times, but that was also fruitless. I tried every way I could think of to quit. I read many self-help books and went to therapy. I just could not let go of that last bottle. The power alcohol had over me was so strong; I was hopeless. I had no idea how I was ever going to take control of my life again.

At my worst I was drinking as much as forty ounces of hard liquor in a single day. The warm feeling of rum or vodka going down my throat after the children had gone to bed was paradise. I could feel the pain and suffering I had felt all day quickly go away. Then for a couple of hours, I was feeling great. I felt good till I passed out. When I was not working, I could drink as soon as I got up in the morning, just to help ease the pain from the hangover from the day before. I usually kept that last drink next to my bed so in the morning I could ease the pain as soon as I got up. I just drank enough to keep me from being sick till the young ones would go to sleep. I always tried to hide my drinking from my children, but most days toward the end I was so hungover they could smell liquor on my breath and could tell I had been drinking. I always tried to spend quality time with them, but in the last few years I was out of control. I am sure that quality time was not so great for them.

On the outside everything looked good. I was a relatively successful adult and doing well socially. Other than my wife, people could not tell how much I was struggling. Some may have noticed I had a drinking problem, but they could not see how bad it really was. It looked like our marriage was doing fine and that I had good children. What was not apparent was the struggle going on inside my head. I had been hurting, struggling with alcoholism for over ten years. It was taking a toll on my health, my marriage, and my children. In the final year of my addiction, I went downhill very fast. Besides addiction, I was also suffering from depression and anxiety without knowing it, and I was treating it with alcohol. Towards the end I could no longer hide behind the bottle. What I thought I was hiding from everyone but my wife was now in the open. My family knew what was going on and that added to my shame.

In the spring of '99 I was blessed with my dream job. I got to work from home. That meant I would no longer have to worry about my coworkers or customers smelling liquor on my breath from the night before. On top of that I was no longer on stand-by for a week every month, for which I had to stay sober. I figured it was perfect, but it made things a lot worst since I could now enjoy the freedom of having a few drinks on the job. That is when things started to spiral downward fast.

On one occasion, after binge drinking during a two-week vacation, the withdrawals were so bad when I returned to work that I had to go to the hospital. I thought it was allergies. The doctor thought I was having a heart attack, but after doing tests, he concluded it was just withdrawals. They kept me sedated in the hospital. They performed a liver biopsy, and to my surprise my liver was in better shape than I expected. It was quite enlarged, but

I did not have any sclerosis. After a week in the hospital, the doctor discharged me and told me he would see me again in a few weeks or months as most drunks always return. Instead of giving me advice on where to seek help, he told me to be a man and quit drinking. I promised myself that I would never be back there. For once, I kept a promise I made to myself and never saw him again, but only because the next time I had to be hospitalized for my drinking, I went to a different hospital for treatment. At least the doc that treated me at the other hospital gave me advice and a referral to therapy. Therapy helped a little but not enough to get me to stop drinking. I really did not know where to turn for help anymore. I was afraid of going to AA meetings because then I would have to admit I was an alcoholic.

Early during my teens and for quite a few years after being married, I would only drink at parties or special occasions. I had always enjoyed a good drink when I was younger but never abused alcohol too much. I had my first drink when I was just fourteen. I had decided to taste the liquor from my dad's bottle and got a really good buzz, so I would drink a few shots every now and then till one day my dad confronted the family to find out who had been drinking his liquor. My dad did not drink very much so the alcohol level should not have been going down. He had marked the bottle and could tell somebody had been drinking it. He never found out that it was me since I had five other siblings, and I think he suspected my older brother. After that when I would take a sip, I would add water to get it back level to the mark. I knew that I could only do that a few times as it was diluting the contents.

I had never planned on becoming an alcoholic, it just gradually happened. I had a really hard time falling asleep at night, so I would drink a few beers before going to bed. Unfortunately after some years, a couple beers was not enough to get me to sleep, so I would have more and more every night. Then eventually instead of beer, I started drinking rum or vodka and in greater quantities.

At age twenty-six I got married and built our house. At the same time I started having a major problem in my right ankle. I had not twisted it or anything; I just woke up one morning with severe tenderness and pain. After a few days, it was not getting any better, so I went to the doctor. After many X-rays I went to see a specialist. After many tests and a few years past, he decided I needed an operation. He was not sure what the problem was, but since it had been about four years and he still couldn't figure out what the cause was, he opted for surgery. I wanted to get it fixed so I went along for the ride. He put a long stainless-steel pin in my foot for support. After the operation my ankle was worse than ever. I could no longer play any sports or do any running at all. Later on, the specialist pulled the pin out of my joint, the doctor told me that he had done all he could to help me, that I was built wrong, and was not normal. He told me not to come and see him again.

A few more years went by and I went to see another specialist for my ankle. The next surgeon did many tests and told me I needed reconstructive surgery. He said that the original problem had been cause by psoriatic arthritis, and I should not have had an operation. So I had a second surgery to reconstruct the joint. After that second surgery, I was able to play hockey again and ride a bicycle, but I still could not do any running. The surgeon also referred me to a rheumatologist who worked on getting my arthritis under control. I also went to see a dermatologist for my psoriasis. As the years went by the arthritis spread to my hands, then my knees, then my hip, and eventually my whole body.

So for years I drank and exercised very little. I told myself I had a great life despite my problems, since I had a wonderful wife, smart children, and a good paying job. What else could a person want? "I have arthritis and I am an alcoholic, but there are many others in this world that are a lot worse than me," I told myself. I was about seventy-five pounds overweight at that time and completely out of shape. Anytime I had a problem, I would deal with it by getting drunk.

It wasn't just the problems that got me drinking. I was also using every excuse that I could to enjoy a beer. Before I worked from home, I was travelling quite a bit for work.

I serviced computer printers for Hewlett Packard, spent a lot of time on the road, and stayed often in hotels. We would sometimes have office parties, or parties at the fire station. After every hockey game we would have beer in the dressing room. If there was no party, I would come up with my own reasons. Maybe I had a pay raise or caught a nice fish on the weekend or had been lucky hunting. So for everything good I was rewarding myself and justifying it with alcohol. Anytime something was not going right I justified drinking to forget about it. After a while, I did not need an excuse anymore. I was just drinking every day.

When I was younger, I always stopped drinking for a month or more every year to prove to myself and my wife that I could control my drinking and that I was not an alcoholic. That worked for quite a few years till one year I could not last a month. Then I could not even stay sober a week.

At one point I figured I would start making my own beer and wine to save money. Well, always having booze at my disposal did not help matters. I could drink more and not feel as guilty taking money away from the family. I also justified my drinking since I was still performing quite well at work, and always had enough money for my children to play sports or other things. I kept telling myself that family always came first no matter what, but I always had to get my fix one way or another. I used all the excuses in the book to justify my drinking. I started to promise Lucille that I would quit after a certain holiday or after my vacations or next year. I always intended to keep those promises, but it never happened. Even though I believed I would do it, I just couldn't because I was no longer in control. Alcohol had taken over my life.

Chapter 2

Detox

Another mental issue was nagging at me. There was a terrible accident one afternoon, a head-on collision where a father was killed and trapped in the front seat. I responded with the fire department but was not yet trained on first-aid. We had to extricate one of the man's daughters over her dad's body. I had felt so helpless and guilty for a long time and for no good reason. I felt like I had done something wrong, but I didn't cause the accident. Still I could not shake it off for so many years till one day I finally talked about it. I was at a training regarding PTSD and decided to open up to another responder. He listened to my story and just that helped me deal with it much better. Before that time it kept me awake quite often when something triggered that memory. Sometimes I wished I had been drinking that day so I would not have responded to that accident. I joined the provincial Critical Incident Stress Management team and stayed on for many years to help when major events occurred in our local area since I knew how valuable talking through trauma could help.

Around this time I told myself I would start to eat healthy and stop drinking when I hit forty. I wanted to spend quality time with my children. I wanted to take control of my life and start having a healthy lifestyle. I wanted to see them graduate, get married, and have children of their own. I started reading a lot of books on organic growing and healthy eating. I also read a lot about alcoholism and the why and how to get better. I figured if I did not change my habits by forty, I would be in a wheelchair by forty-five, that is if I was still alive. The pain from arthritis was so severe in the morning that I could hardly get out of bed or climb out of the car when I reached work. That is when I discovered a variety of foods that were very bad for my arthritis: red meat, tomatoes, and grapefruit, among other foods. So I changed my diet and medication. My arthritis improved, but I was still a mess mentally. My thinking was actually getting worse. I was in a very bad place. Lucille and I knew that if I kept drinking, I would eventually be fired from my job, and we would lose everything. She was very worried most of the time, knowing I was out of control by then.

The struggle was real, and I could not see any glimmer of hope. I was willing to go for therapy, but that did not help a lot. I tried to quit drinking with my doctor's help and medication. I did not know what else to try and was willing to do anything. I was very sad and hopelessness consumed me. Many times, I thought about ending my life, making it look like an accident, to make it easier on my wife and children, but I really did not want that. In the back of my mind I always thought I could stop drinking. I really believed that I could.

My life was usually filled with enough excitement to keep me busy. With my wonderful wife we raised four children. I had a good career in IT as a system's engineer with a decent company. It was a good profession, and I received a fair salary. I stayed with the company for thirty-four years, till they offered me an early retirement. I always had a good performance at work and was well rewarded with good raises. I traveled quite a bit for my work, mostly within North America. I also had to be on stand-by one week per month, which meant if there was a problem at work at any hour of the night, they expected me to come take care of the issue. So that one week I had to avoid drinking or at least stay sober enough to be able to drive to the office. One weekend when I was on stand-by, I had a few too many drinks when I got a callout. Since I was in no shape to drive, I had to get a colleague to cover for me. I told him I was sick and could not respond. He covered for me, but somehow our boss found out about it. At 8 a.m. the next Monday morning, the manager called me in his office to check up on me. I had not had a drink since Saturday night, so I got away with it that time.

I also had many hobbies; I enjoyed hunting and fishing or anything that I could do to be outside. I had built an outdoor rink, so the kids could enjoy skating and play hockey. I also spend time snowshoeing or cross country skiing in the winter and fishing and canoeing in the summer. I liked to go on day hikes, but never did an overnight backpacking trip before I was sixty years old. I had taken a survival and orienteering course in my twenties and had spent a night alone in the wilderness without any tent or gear. That night it had gone below freezing, and I had to build a lean to and a fire to keep me warm. I didn't sleep much that night because I had to keep the fire going. It was an awesome experience that I'll never forget. We would also go alpine skiing once or twice every winter as a family. It was a lot of fun, but we couldn't afford to go too often.

What I was most passionate about was the fire department. I am a volunteer firefighter with over thirty-six years of experience. I started as a firefighter then became the training officer for over twenty years. I was also deputy chief for a number of years and even fire chief for over a year. I took over when the village council did not want to renew the contract with the fire chief at the time. I did that for a while but being chief was not for me. I enjoyed the respect of my fellow firefighters, but there was way too much politics. As a fire department we respond on average around 250 alarms per year and that includes medical calls and motor vehicle accidents. For a volunteer fire department that is busy. There is no ambulance service within the village, so the ambulance has to respond from the nearest town, twenty to thirty minutes away. We also cover a very busy stretch of the Trans Canada highway, and we see many serious motor vehicle crashes. In just one year we had seven fatal accidents with eleven fatalities.

That year we decided to raise money to purchase the Jaws of Life. I chaired a committee with a goal to raise twenty thousand dollars in two years. In five months we had managed to get over fifty-five thousand dollars and were able to buy the Jaws of Life and a rescue vehicle. A couple of years later the government divided the highway, so the accidents and fatalities went down by quite a bit. Being on call twenty-four seven kept me sober quite a bit more in the early years. We have a policy not to respond to an alarm if you have been drinking, so if I wanted to respond I had to avoid drinking. My children really enjoyed spending Saturday nights at the fire station when they were young. I would go and prepare for the Monday night training, and they would run around the trucks. Three of my children were at one time also volunteer firefighters. One of them is now a career firefighter, so it was probably a good influence on him.

On that cold December afternoon all hope had faded away. I had to end the suffering. I had been in a crash and totaled my truck two days before, so I was now without a vehicle. I felt I had nothing left. I got a piece of paper and wrote a note to my wife and children begging them to forgive me. I told them I loved them very much. Then I started to look for a way to end it without suffering too much. With all the gun, knives, and pills gone, the only way was to set my house on fire. My wife had locked the garage so I could not get access the gasoline. She had also taken the keys of the ATV, so I could not go to the store. I knew I could set a fire with paper on the stove but that it would probably drive me out of the house when the smoke got too thick, and it would also leave my children without a house. I was not okay with that.

What happened next is a blur. I woke up and my parents were at the door. I thought "at last, my dad will lend me his truck and then I can at least go to the liquor store and figure out my next plan." To my surprise, in my mind at least, even my parents let me down. He told me he would lend me the truck after I got my life in order. What I thought was a bad situation was about to turn worse. Lucille, looking for my best interest, had called the police. They showed up and found the note I had written earlier. I personally knew both cops, having worked with them with the fire department. They told my parents they could leave, that they had things under control. I told them I was in my own house and unless they were charging me with a crime, they had to leave. According to them I was a threat to myself, and they were taking me to jail. I still don't know why they locked me up rather than take me to the hospital. That was probably the worst four to six hours of my life. I was hurting so much from withdrawal and shame. They had stripped me of anything that I could use to hurt myself. After spending what seemed like an eternity there, another brother in-law showed up and told them to take me to the hospital. I still don't know how he even knew I was there since I had not called anybody.

They kept me at the psychiatric ward at the hospital overnight and gave me medication to seduce me. The next morning I saw a psychiatrist and convinced him that I was not suicidal, that I was just suffering from withdrawal. He questioned me for about two hours and said if my wife was okay to pick me up, I could go home. I am not sure what he told my wife, but she took me back home. I promised her one more time that I would quit drinking but that she needed to ween me off slowly. She was skeptical but seemed to understand. She told me the kids were staying at her mother's place and that she would help wean me off the alcohol. Alter two days my kids returned home to my delight. I promised them I would stop drinking soon.

After a few weeks I agreed to go to the detox center. She had already made all the arrangement behind my back. She said that was the only option. That first day in detox was even worse than the day in jail, but for the first time in years I could see a small light like a candle at the far end of a tunnel. All weeks have seven days, but that week in detox seem like it was the longest week in my life. Lucille and children came to visit. I felt so ashamed but could see they were prouder of me than ever before. I attended my first AA meeting at the detox center and got a twenty-four-hour badge and then a three-day badge. After seven days I came home to my wonderful, supportive family. The day I came home, I was more scared than I had ever been in my life.

My youngest daughter was a very accomplished athlete and had won a lot of medals, but when I got home and gave her those two badges, she said it was the best medals she ever got. Those are the only medals I got because I stopped going to AA. I don't see anything wrong with AA. I think it's a great organization and has helped so many recovering alcoholics. It just wasn't right for me. I needed some other method of coping. I also had a few appointments with my doctor to help me with my sleeping disorder. He diagnosed me with idiopathic insomnia, a sleeping disorder that starts when you're a child. He gave me a sleeping medication and reassured me it was not addictive. He said it was habit forming and it was better that I slept than tried to cope with lack of sleep with alcohol.

Chapter 3
Sober

On the way home from the detox center I was terrified. I thought, "How am I going to get through this?" Lucille assured me she would be there with me every step of the way, and I sure needed her support. The first month, alcohol was all I could think about. It was on my mind every single minute I was awake. I was struggling hard to stay sober, however, I was determined. I stayed awake at night. I was hurting bad, but my eyes were no longer blood shot and my face was not as red as it used to be. My mind was clearing. I used to always make sure I knew where my next drink was coming from. Now I thought about how to avoid that next drink. Sometimes the cravings were so severe I had to tell myself I could go another minute and then re-evaluate the situation. I had to switch my behavior drastically. At first, I stayed in my bedroom and played video games or do crosswords puzzle. I did anything to occupy my brain.

That first month I was very anti-social. Things started to be a little bit better and then I hit another struggle.

Before the alcohol covered all my emotions. When sober, I started to feel guilty and remorseful over what I had done to Lucille and the children. I cried at night even though I was sober. Knowing that I was now doing good and making everybody happy kept me from falling again. I could tell that my family was forgiving me more than I was forgiving myself, and I sure needed that. Without their support I would have so easily taken that first drink.

Feeling I was cured, in late spring of 2000, I had a family meeting and told them I thought I could handle a social drink since I had been sober for a few months. They were not convinced, but I told them if I get drunk once, I will go right back into detox. Less than five days later I was back in detox because they were right and I could not control myself. That time I only spend four days as I convinced the counselors I was good to go back home since I had only been drinking for a few days, and could see how wonderful the sober life was.

From then on, I knew that if I have one drink, I am gone. I avoided any place that could lead me into temptation. My parents were aware of my problem, and if we had family reunion even with just my brothers and sisters, there was no alcohol if I was going to attend. I felt bad, but I knew they were doing it for me. In the fall I went back to playing hockey, but that was another struggle since everybody had a beer after the games. I would get undressed as fast possible and would leave the locker room before anyone would invite me for a drink.

Around that time my arthritis was also getting better probably because alcohol made it worse, and I was taking a new drug to get it under control. While I was drinking, I never felt good unless I was drunk, and I was not eating properly since my stomach was never settled. Once I got sober, I was eating much healthier and probably absorbing the nutrients better also. As the weeks and months passed, I was starting to look very positively at life. Slowly the shame subsided, and the cravings were further apart. I was finally starting to feel good about myself and I was also spending quality time with my family.

I bought a new bicycle and got hooked on mountain biking. I could go on long bike rides with the kids, with friends, or on my own. Going for a three- to four-hour drive was real therapy when I was craving a drink. I had swapped a bad addiction for a good one. I switch from an addiction that was quickly killing me to one that was making me better. On top of the benefit of exercise, I was getting great therapy from spending a lot of time outdoors. In the winter, when I could not bike, I snowshoed or cross-country skied. I became hooked on exercise, and it was a good thing.

The light at the end of the tunnel was getting brighter every day. Being sober, I had found something I had been searching many years. I had found that small amber of light at the end of that long tunnel. I was getting healthier, spending a lot less time in the doctor's office and at the hospital. I started to feel really good about myself and started to even race mountain bikes. I still wanted to drink, but the struggle was getting easier every day. Whenever I was really getting bad cravings, I would go on extra-long rides in the forest sometimes for six or seven hours. When I got home the cravings were not as strong. Lucille was also a great encouragement. She took all the money I used to spend on booze and bought me something I wanted, so I could see that it was worth quitting. Between nature, exercise, and my family support, I was on my way to healing. The time I spent with my children was now better for me and for them.

After almost twenty years of not being able to jog or run, I could finally try to jog. I was now in great shape from the mountain biking I was doing every day. That first year of biking after getting sober I had peddled almost six thousand miles. My first attempt at running, though, was a disaster. All I could do was a quarter mile before the pain in my knee was so bad I had to stop. My younger brother, Bert, had raced a 10k and had inspired me to do the same. I struggled for about a month of severe knee pain trying to do my first mile run nonstop. I wanted to run so badly that I would keep on trying even if I was suffering. I told myself if I could stop drinking, I could run a mile. After all, as bad as the pain was, it was not as hard as quitting drinking. Finally after a month or so I could run a mile without any pain, and to my surprise something strange happened. The more I ran, the less pain I had. My rheumatologist told me not to run more than three miles as it was bad for my joints with all the pounding for a person with arthritis.

Three years after having my last drink I started running more and more almost every day. About a month after running my first mile, I did my first 5k race. I pushed way too hard. I thought I was going to have a heart attack, but I enjoyed the thrill of completing that first race. A month after that first 5k race I was finally ready to register in my first 10k race like my brother. That first race I started way too fast and cramped really bad. I did manage to finish, though, and was hooked. I did not stop there, so I looked for a longer race and found a 25k in Prince Edward Island. Still that wasn't quite enough so five months after my first painful mile I ran my first marathon in under four hours at the age of forty-seven.

Instead of being in a wheelchair at forty-five I ran a marathon at forty-seven. It was a small and beautiful fall race in Nova Scotia called the Harvest Valley Marathon. On race day the weather was perfect and all the leaves were in full color. The course was set up along a curvy rolling country road. That was one of my favorite races and a day I will always cherish. I had completed a full marathon knowing that only a few years before walking to the store was a real struggle. I had done something that I never, ever thought I would be able or want to do. It was real, and I felt so proud of my accomplishment. I figured nothing could stop me now. My son drove me home because I was in so much pain, but I was happy, it was a good pain. I remember stopping at a service station on the way home to go to the washroom, and it took me almost ten minutes to get out of the car. He had to drive as close to the door as possible.

That weekend I also bought a road bike so that when it was too muddy on the trails in the forest I could ride on the road. I did most of my running or biking in the wood since the wilderness is such good therapy. As I mentioned before, I think nature has some great healing power. But sometimes other unexpected thing happens while mountain biking or running in the woods. I found some very strange object that did not belong in the woods.

One day about ten miles from the nearest road, I found a golf cart that somebody had stolen and had gone for a joy ride. They probably had a long walk home after they got stuck in the mud and left the cart there. Another time on another long bike ride, I saw a cube van in a place where it definitely did not belong. It was backed off a side trail, and I could see fresh tire tracks in the mud. I could not see any driver or passenger in the front, but I could tell that the back doors were opened. I had no idea what to expect as I cautiously approached the van. To my surprise, behind the van in the woods was an automated teller machine that had been busted wide open. There was no cash left in the machine and nobody was around, so I reported the incident to the police. Apparently, the vehicle had been stolen the night before and the thieves drove through a business front window and grabbed the money machine. They had force it open and had dumped it with the van in the forest.

My favorite story happened one day on a long run along the Petitcodiac River in Memramcook. As I was running on a trail a shad about two feet in length mysteriously dropped from the sky missing me by just couple of inches. The fish was still alive and flopping back and forth on the ground. I looked up and saw the bald eagle had dropped it next to me. I am not sure if he took pity of me and wanted to feed me because I looked so bad on that long run or maybe he lost his grip and dropped the fish just above my head. I had many other encounters with wildlife, through the years: bears, moose, hawks, snakes, but that one is still my favorite. That may be where the saying comes from its raining fish.

I kept on racing about a marathon per year. I didn't properly train, so I kept getting injured, but nothing serious. The rheumatologist was supportive since the longer I ran the less pain I got, unless I got injured of course. He finally told me that since running helped me with my arthritis I might as well run as much as I wanted to. Those long runs and bike rides alone for hours did a lot for my arthritis and was really the driving force that kept me sober in the early years. The suffering after a two-hour run was so much more rewarding than a day of suffering after a night of drinking. I finally believed I was on the right path of healing. I was always looking for the next challenge. I always tried to push myself to the next limit. I went on to complete seven marathons before I retired.

I wish I could say everything with my life was finally going great, but I had not noticed things were not so well with my wife. All the years of my drinking had taken a toll on her. Around the time of my recovery she lost her dad to a heart attack, and her sister succumbed to cancer. She had dealt with her sister's struggle for two years before she passed, and it was hard on Lucille. Then her mother had a heart attack and had to have open heart surgery. Lucille was the only sibling in her family that did not have a permanent job at that time, so she took care of her mother.

All the years that the children were growing up Lucille had stayed at home to raise them. Now with the kids getting older and with all the problems she had faced, her own struggle started. She also managed our finances when I was drinking, and I let her manage them after I got sober. I was not aware that we were spending way too much money on my hobbies and we were getting into financial trouble. I thought everything was good, but once again, our marriage was going sideways without me noticing it. Suddenly we were drifting apart. She had been taking care of everybody and everything, but nobody took care of her or even noticed she was struggling.

I tried the best that I could to support her, since she had supported me for so many years. She got back into the workforce after many years. It helped us financially, but she needed more. She had some sort of PTSD. I loved her very much, and it was finally time to take care of her. The children and I helped with her healing as best we could.

Being sober changed my life in so many ways. I was able to pay attention to my marriage, and it got back on track after some time. I also got a lot more productive at work. I was even asked to go deliver training in Bangalore, India for a new center that Hewlett Packard was opening. I had to create my own course material and traveled several times abroad to train others. There is no way ten years earlier I ever would have been called upon to do something like that. Since getting sober, I have been able to conquer so much that running a marathon or traveling to India to train people seems like minor endeavors. My family life and quality time with my children got so much better as the years past, and I was finally living the life I wanted to. Drinking took so many years away from my life that I will never be able to get back. That is all behind me, and now I intended to live life to the fullest. I was given a second chance on life.

For about eight years I volunteered with the Canadian Ski Patrol. The first year that I was a ski patrol, I was selected rookie of the year. I became one of the instructors and taught for a few years. A few of us, patrollers, received a lifesaving award after we responded to a snowmobile accident close to the resort after the skier collided with a tree. He was in really bad shape, and we kept him alive and brought him out to the ambulance.

Work was going great but then the company started to go sideways. What used to be one of the best companies to work for was becoming a real challenge. Many of my friends and co-workers were losing their jobs. Moral was bad. One day they offered early retirement to longtime employees. I was not quite ready to retire but was afraid of what might come next, so I accepted the offer and retired at age fifty-eight in November 2013. Now I was without a job and worried about what I was going to do next.

Chapter 4

Retired

After I retired, I looked at it as a new beginning, a new chapter in my life. I didn't want to just end my career and then slowly fade away in a senior's home. I had recently built a nice camp where I had planned to spend my retirement. I always thought I would spend my retirement sitting on the front porch in a rocking chair with a big cigar and a glass of whisky. That was my dream when I was younger. But by the time I retired I did not smoke, and I no longer drank. I wanted to do more than sit in front of the TV all day or go bowling, play cards or darts, or shoot pool like most of the people I went to school with. There is nothing wrong with that, but that was not for me. I had to come up with a plan. I bought a nice high-end camera and decided I was going to take up photography. I took many nice shots of nature but did not have the patience for getting the best shots, so I had to get another plan.

My dad died of Alzheimer's rotting away in a senior's home where nobody was even aware of who they were let alone their own name. It was a horrible site to see such a smart man lose his mind. After he retired, he did some gardening at home, delivered meals to seniors, played darts, played golf, and joined a few bowling leagues. My dad was great in my eyes. I loved him, but his lifestyle was not the kind of life I wanted after retirement. I find many people retire and believe that they are too old to do anything. For me I got a second chance at life in my forty's and plan to live it to the fullest. Maybe it's because of my alcoholism or because I got my arthritis under control that I am optimist, but for me life does not end at sixty; it's just a new era.

My best fishing buddy and I used to go out fishing or hunting anytime we could. He retired at sixty and wanted to devote his life to fishing and spending times outdoors. However, after he retired, he took on a part-time job and did even less fishing than he did when he was working full-time. Around age sixty-four he was diagnosed with cancer and his life was fading fast. On a fall fishing trip that he suspected would be his last, he told me he regretted not having spent more time enjoying his favorite hobby. I was still working at the time and told myself I would not be like him when my turn came to retire. He got a second chance at life and survived his cancer, but as strange as it may seem, he is now in his early seventies and is still working part-time and hardly fishes anymore. He tells me he spends most of his time watching TV in the winter time waiting for spring to come so that he can go fishing, but he never comes out anymore.

I wanted more out of life when I retired, so I decided I was going to complete an Ironman Triathlon, which is a 2.4-mile swim, 112-mile bike ride, and a 26.22-mile run. I registered for the Ironman and really had no idea what it was all about, but figured if other people could do it, then certainly I could do it also. I knew that to do an Ironman you had to swim, and since I could not swim, I had to learn to swim and had to learn fast. I had less than nine months to go from swimming ten to fifteen yards in a shallow pool to be able to swim over two miles in a lake. I joined two beginner swim groups to try to get as many lessons and as much practice as I could. I also bought a membership at a local aqua center.

Since I had no idea how to train for such an event, I figured I needed a coach to help me with this journey and got a local coach that could help me. Swimming did not come as easy as I expected. I struggled a lot, coming home after every session very frustrated. If I had not already registered for the Ironman, I would have quit swimming after a couple weeks. It was hard; I was not making the progress needed to swim the distance. My swim coach was very encouraging, but I knew I was not going to make it. I was heading for failure, but he kept pushing me and telling me I could do it.

Both my swim coach and my Ironman coach convinced me to register in an Olympic distance triathlon along the way in June which consist of a 0.9-mile swim, followed by a 24.8-mile bike ride and a 10k run. It would be a great way to tell if I was ready for the Ironman. I was ready for the biking and running, but the swimming was a different story. To make things worse I got part pneumonia and was sick for two weeks before the race, I even had to get antibiotics. Normally it's best to get some open water practice before doing your first race. It is also a good practice to try out your wet suit in a controlled environment. I was not able to do either because I had been sick.

The Olympic triathlon was awful. I was hyperventilating during the whole swim portion of the race; my wetsuit was way too tight; I had real hard time breathing. I was hurting badly, but I figured I was going to finish since I wanted to get through the swim and then quit this foolish plan of mine. Everybody was out of the water long before me. I was dead last, but I did finish, and I was still alive. The bike ride was also horrible because I was still suffering from the swim. I had swallowed a lot of water and was nauseated, and I could not get my heart to stop pounding and was cursing my coach. I did manage to complete the race but was not happy with my experience. I was nauseated and was feeling very sick.

Both my swim coach and my Ironman coach were at the race and were happy with my performance. It had been my worst race ever. I told them, "Well, I guess that's it. I now know that I cannot do an Ironman this year." They both said on the contrary I just proved that I could do it". I was not so sure. With only two months left of training and the way I felt that day after the race, I was almost certain I could not complete an Ironman that year. But what the hell, I had already paid my entry fee and booked the motel in Mont Tremblant; I figured I would use that race as a training experience so that in a year or so I would be able to actually complete an Ironman.

That summer I spent a lot of time swimming in a lake all by myself. I bought an inflatable buoy that I would drag in case I got in trouble. I was swimming about two miles nonstop before I got to the Ironman race that August morning. The longest bike ride I had completed was about seventy-five miles, and the longest training run had been thirteen miles.

On a cool windy August morning in 2014, when I was fifty-nine years old and terrified of what I was going to do all day, I found myself at 5 a.m. surrounded by twenty-five hundred athletes at Mont Tremblant in Quebec. The lake was choppy, I was alone in a crowd, and I was scared even though there were many lifeguards along the course. I wanted to run away somewhere and hide. I knew only one thing: I was about to suffer and suffer a lot that day. I was hoping I would not die, but told myself, if I can stop drinking, I can do this.

The swim began and I started to get kicked and pushed around by other swimmers. I was looking for clear water but there were people everywhere. I was struggling but was thinking one stroke at the time, the same as I did when I stopped drinking. At first, I thought I wouldn't drink one minute at a time, then one hour at a time and then one day, one month, one year. So concentrating on one stroke at a time, I finally made it to the halfway mark. Well, if I can do half, I thought, there is nothing to stop me from doing the other half, so I pushed on. I swallowed a lot of water and was not feeling great. That was one of the hardest things I had ever done, but I did manage to complete the swim in a little over one and a half hour. I was exhausted but so happy. I had done something that I would never had imagine I could do in my life or even a couple months before.

I thought the worst was over, but I was so wrong. After the swim I had to change and bike 112 miles in the mountains and then I had to run a marathon. It took me a long time to get ready to start the bike portion of the race, but I was happy I had completed the swim and had not drowned or been pulled out of the race. I am not sure which one would have been worse. The first sixty miles of biking was not so bad. I managed to keep a good pace, but the day was starting to get long. I ate well on the bike as I had been doing in practice, but the last fifty miles were a struggle. Muscles that I did not know I had were hurting. I had done the training and was confident at that time that I could succeed, but as the miles went up so did the doubt. To top it off I got hit with a heavy downpour in the last six miles of the ride. My family was there for support. I could not let them down, so I had to push on. I finished the bike portion to the cheers of my family, but I was beat, wet, and busted. After more than nine hours of pushing myself, I still had to run a marathon. At that time I figured I had about eight hours to complete the marathon before being pulled off the course, so unless I get hurt, I figured, I should be able to complete it.

To finish a marathon is hard enough when well rested and properly fueled with carbs, but after swimming almost two and a half miles and biking over a hundred miles, it's extra hard. The first ten miles of the run was not too bad except for a few heavy downpours that hit again. My socks were wet, and I had very big blisters with over fifteen miles to go. At that point the pain was intense. When you are so exhausted and in pain, the mind starts playing games on you. It's easy to go into a very dark place, with lots of time to think about your life. I was hurting so much by the time I reached twenty-one miles; every muscle was tired, but I knew at that point I was going to finish. My dad was at a nursing home with Alzheimer's at the time and I thought how much he would be proud of me if he could understand what I was about to accomplish, especially considering from where I had come. I was very sad for him, but he actually helped me get to the finish line. What an awesome feeling to hear that voice on the microphone saying Louis Cormier, YOU. ARE. AN IRONMAN.

I had completed my first Ironman in fourteen hours and thirty minutes. My original goal was to complete it before the cut off time of seventeen hours, but then I revised it to try to do it under fifteen hours. Although I was so tired that even the tips of my hair were exhausted, I was very happy with my results. I thanked my family for support. I was so glad I had stopped drinking years before. I felt so blessed to have my health. Many of my school-age friends were suffering from heart problems, diabetes, or other health issues.

After a short rest and getting some electrolytes and potassium, I felt rejuvenated enough to go back out and cheer the last finishers who were coming in just before the midnight cut-off time. I was so emotional, knowing what they were going through, how much they were hurting. That night was I was so confident and proud of myself. When we went to bed, I asked my wife, "How does it feel to sleep with an Ironman?"

"You are the same man that you were last night and on top of that you are completely exhausted," she replied.

I wasn't expecting that amusing comment. She certainly put things in perspective and me in my place.

I went on to compete in my second Ironman the following year in Whistler, British Columbia. It was another tough swim with a mass of swimmers that started in the water at the same time. It was a very windy and cold day. When I got out of the water, I was nauseated from being bounced by the big waves and swallowing water. The temperature was about forty-six degrees Fahrenheit at the start of the bike portion. It was raining hard, and by the time I got to the top of the mountain the precipitation had turn to wet snow. Quite a few of the participants quit at that time because they were hypothermic. I ended up completing the race in under fourteen hours, beating my previous time by over thirty-five minutes.

Later that year a group of women approached me to discuss organizing a race. Most of them worked in the schools and were concerned that many children were going to school during the winter not very well dressed. We have really harsh winters here in New Brunswick. This is not a rich province, but most families are doing okay. However some less fortunate kids go to school with no winter jacket, boots, mitts, or tuque. They have to stay inside during recreation times because they don't have proper clothes. That group of women had started to knit mittens and tuques to help dress those school children from kindergarten to grade eight. They were having a hard time raising money to buy wool. They thought a race might help raise the funds needed. As it turned out, I had been thinking about organizing a road race in Memramcook. I wanted to give people an incentive to get in shape. I knew how getting in shape helped save my life and wanted to give back to the community a gift that I had received.

So after a few meetings we approached the village directors to see if they would be onboard with a fund-raiser race. They were supportive and said they could help us with the infrastructure. So I took on the challenge of being a race organizer, and we set the race date for early May 2016. We had one-hundred-meter and six-hundred-meter kids races for preschool kids. The main races were the 5k and 10k runs. The citizens of Memramcook were very supportive. We got some great sponsors and over seventy-five volunteers on race day. On race day the weather was gorgeous, and we had over two hundred racers participate. The committee worked very hard and our first annual race was a success. We raised over six thousand dollars and were able to buy complete snowsuits, including boots, for quite a few children. My mom was eight-four years old that year, and she walked the 5k. My sister, who had never ran a race before, ran her first 5k. She went on to complete a half marathon two years later. Seeing the smiles on everyone's faces after the race and knowing that I had helped many people get out and walk or run was quite gratifying.

In 2017, our second year, we added a half marathon. We had more support from everybody, but the weather did not cooperate. On race day, we had over three hundred racers registered, but because of the heavy rain and strong wind, some racers did not show up. Everybody who did show up for the race had a great time. Quite a few racers thanked me and said I was the driving force that got them to get in shape and walk or run their first 5k or 10k. Knowing that I helped was a great reward, and on top that, we were able to raise over ten thousand dollars to dress even more children. Just a few years before, I would never have believed I could help so many people when as a drunk, I could not even help myself.

The third year of the race, I was away hiking the Appalachian Trail, but I managed to get a good replacement for race director. I worked with the committee to help organize up until spring when I left for my hike. Again, the weather didn't cooperate. The strong winds knocked some electrical wires down on the road, and they had to reroute the race at the last minute. But I think it was still a success.

I had come a long way in the past 18 years. I went from drinking every night to a month sober, to a year sober, to not being able to swim and then to completing four Ironman Triathlons, finishing my last one in under thirteen hours. While I don't have much of a bucket list—probably because I didn't think I'd live that long—I have always wanted to know what it would be like to live homeless for several months in the wilderness. I never thought it would happen, but when I decided to hike the Appalachian Trail, I knew that one of my few dreams would come true.

Chapter 5

Katahdin

My older brother, Gilles, had been asking me for a long time to hike the Fundy Footpath. It's a three- to five-day backpacking trip along the Bay of Fundy in the wilderness of New Brunswick. In 2015, at the age of sixty, I finally gave in. The trail has gained popularity in recent years, but even that year they told us at the registration desk that only seventy-five people had registered to hike the whole trail that year. That's not to say only seventy-five people hiked the whole trail. Even though registration is required on both ends of the trailheads, some folks don't register.

The trail goes up and down a lot of ravines. There are many very steep climbs and descents with slippery roots and rocks. Since I had always enjoyed the wilderness, I had a blast. It was tough carrying a backpack for the first time in my life but sleeping outdoors and building a campfire at night was fantastic. I was in great shape after having just completed an Ironman a few weeks before, so I did not find it too difficult. Gilles was quite tired, but he was elated to have accomplished that hike. I had heard about thirty years ago about a real long hiking trail in the States, but did not know the name. I thought it was called the Adirondack trail. I told him that we should hike it the next year. Well after a bit of research I found out it was called the Appalachian Trail and it was over two thousand miles and it would take at least four to six months to complete. Gilles said he would love to do it but couldn't be away that long. I figured I would have to wait to enjoy such a challenge, but the more I read about the trail, the hungrier I got.

In the fall of 2015, I went alone on a three-day backpack trip on the Chignecto Trail in Nova Scotia. The following year, in 2016, after my fourth Ironman, I hiked the Fundy Footpath again, this time with my younger daughter, Natalie. It took us four days to complete that trip because we got over two inches of rain on the second night, and the next morning the brooks were impassable. We had to wait a whole day in our tents for the rain to stop. We both got blisters from hiking in wet shoes. Nat had never hiked before, but even two days of rain and blisters did not deter her. She also was hooked on hiking and backpacking after that trip. I repeated the Chignecto trip again in 2016.

During that time, I mentioned to some friends my idea of hiking the entire Appalachian Trail (AT). I figured they might think it was a crazy idea, but to my surprise a few friends said it had always been one of their dreams too. More people knew about the trail and had read stories about it than I thought. But most of my friends said it was a dream that would probably never happen. Even so everybody was very encouraging and suggested I should do it. What surprised me the most was when I told Lucille I was thinking of hiking the AT she did not called me crazy. She asked how long a hike it was and wanted to know more details about the trail like how safe it was. I told her it was pretty safe and that I thought it was a two- to three-month hike. She actually told me if you really want to hike the trail, go for it. Lucille said it would be a reward for staying sober all these years and that she was okay with it as long as I stayed safe. What I didn't know was the trek usually takes five to seven months for most.

During this time, one of my sons, Kevin, asked me to go climb up Mount Katahdin, the highest mountain in Maine at 5,367 feet. It's also the northern terminus of the Appalachian Trail. So on October 2, 2017, my daughter, Nat, joined Kevin and me at Baxter State Park where we stayed the night at Katahdin Stream campground. We proceeded to summit the next morning on the Hunt Trail. The weather was nice that morning. We got up very early to give us enough time to climb to the top and come back down before nighttime. Climbing for over five miles to the top was very challenging and the weather on top was cold and cloudy, but it was a great adventure. Nat was scared of the height and wanted to turn back halfway, but Kevin finally convinced her to keep going.

The view on the way up was breathtaking. When we got to the top, the clouds had moved in and we did not have any view at all. It was also quite windy and cold, so we only stayed on the summit for about five minutes, enough time to snap a few pictures before coming back down. At the time I preferred hiking in the woods to climbing a mountain. The descent was just as challenging as the climb, but we made it safely to the bottom. We took the Abol Stream Trail on the way down for some different scenery but that meant when we reached the bottom, we were about five miles from our car. That's when I witnessed my first trail magic. A complete stranger offered to drive Nat and another couple back to our campsite to get our car so she could come pick us up.

That was the first time I had climbed a mountain; it was really rewarding and emotional, especially since I knew I may be doing the whole thing next year. I met a few thru hikers finishing their north bound hike and talked to them about their hike. When I mentioned to my kids I was interested in hiking the entire AT, they encouraged me to just do it. So the next morning I registered in Baxter State Park (BSP) to do the thru hike. According to the Appalachian Trail Council, it is considered a thru hike if you complete the trail within twelve consecutive months. I was now committed to doing it. The next morning we hiked the rest of the trail in the BSP so that way I could start my south bound hike anytime I wanted and not have to worry about BSP being closed since they normally close the park on October 15.

In November 2017, I set out to hike the rest of Maine going southbound. I would get back on the trail for the rest starting in May 2018. The part in Maine is a hundred miles between two towns. It's the longest stretch of the AT without population and is considered very hazardous and challenging. Doing the hundred miles of wilderness alone in late November was not a great plan. I had read there was no problem with phone reception, but I did not have any for most of the time. The days are very short, and the nights are cold and long. On top of that, a couple days before I set out a hurricane had passed through Maine. It had raised the brooks and rivers to dangerous levels. The storm had also taken down so many trees that you had to get completely off trail to continue hiking.

I had arranged for an outfitter to pick me up in Millinocket Maine where I left my car, and he dropped me off at the trailhead. He was also going to drop off half of my food supply on a hunting road halfway along the trail. Unfortunately when I got there my food was nowhere to be found. I still had four days to go with only one day of food left. I had no phone reception, so I was not able to contact him. After about three hours of searching, I decided to abort the hike and follow the hunting road back to a main road. Luckily after about an hour, a couple of hunters came by on a four-wheel drive and offered me a lift. When we got to the top of the hill, they had phone reception, and I could contact the outfitter. He said he had not expected me at the halfway mark till later in the afternoon and that he would bring me my food. I had lost a half day of hiking and my food supply was low since I had only taken seven days of food instead of the recommended ten. That night I was very tired mentally and physically.

Not only were the brooks and river very high, they were also extremely cold. At one such crossing the rope used for crossing was broken. I ended up slipping on a rock and fell in over my head and lost one of my trekking poles. I was soaked through, but my gear in my backpack was in waterproof bags at least. It was raining hard, so I was very concerned I might get hypothermia. It was around four in the afternoon and getting dark. I hiked fast and hard to warm up and then quickly set up my tent so I had time to change into dry clothes for the night and get into my sleeping bag to try to stay warm. I survived the night but the next morning all my wet clothes were frozen. I had to thaw my clothes before putting them on since I had to keep one set of clothes dry for nights.

Because I was running low on food and the days were short, I decided to start before sunrise one morning. About an hour after daylight, I came upon a road that I had crossed the day before and realized I was going the wrong direction. I lost two hours and had to hike an extra four miles to get back on track. After getting back on the trail I came to a river that was three times wider and deeper than the one that I fell in. However this time there was a rope and the water current was a lot slower. The rope was very flimsy, but I managed to make it through safely.

Hiking a hundred miles in sheer wilderness was a new experience for me. It was cold with most nights dropping below freezing. I was unaware there were so many mountains in the east and so many beautiful lakes that they call ponds. Along the way I met a few thru hikers who were finishing their northbound hike. I saw a lot of wild game. One night, about ten minutes before reaching my campsite, I saw a huge bear that weighed probably over four hundred pounds. I had seen a lot of bears before in my life, but that was the biggest I had ever seen in the wild. I was concerned he was so close to where I was tenting, so I made sure I hung my food quite high and away from my tent. Going over White Caps I could see Mount Katahdin; it was so beautiful.

When I finally got to the trailhead after seven days, I hitched a ride into Monson. I got a ride quite fast with a nice guy. He was surprised to see somebody hiking in late November. He was an experienced hiker and suggested that I wait till spring to continue on south. He said the mountains in southern Maine and the Whites in New Hampshire were very dangerous. A cold front with snow storm was coming. I had arranged to stay at the hostel for the night and was going to continue the next morning after restocking. The folks at the hostel all advised me not to proceed since I was not experienced in winter hiking, so I decided to get a shuttle back to my car and head home. I had not made it as far as I wanted to, but the journey was not over, and I had gained great experience. I had told Lucille I would stay safe, and it did not sound like it was safe to continue till spring. That was not the hardest thing I had done, but it was by far the most exiting adventure of my life up to that point.

A week alone in the wilderness gives a person a lot of time to reflect on the value of life; I discovered a new spark in me that I did not know before. I reflected on my childhood and how much I loved my family. I also realized that we were on the earth for a short time, and we should do the most we can while we still have the chance. I had found a new passion and could barely wait till spring to continue on my journey.

Chapter 6

The Preparation

The Appalachian Trail is 2,190 miles long and stretches from Georgia to Maine in the United States and travels along the Appalachian Mountains. It goes through fourteen states and has almost 465,000 feet of elevation climb. I decided to hike the trail alone, so I could go at my own pace and spend time reflecting on life. I knew being alone would push me more outside my comfort zone, but I was also okay with friends or family members joining me for various sections along the way. This adventure was going to be one of the biggest and most challenging undertakings in my life. As I was waiting for spring, I was restless and anxious. At first, I planned to start in Monson, Maine, in late May and go south to Georgia, but then I switched my plans and decided to start on Springer Mountain in Georgia and head back north to Monson.

As soon as I had no more doubt about going; I started to research gear. I already had everything I needed for a week long hike, but I wanted the right gear for a much longer hike. I wanted to go as light as I could so that it would be much easier on my lower joints. Throughout the winter I acquired new and lighter gear to get ready for spring. I spent more money than I had expected, but I wanted to go as light as possible to give me a better chance of success. It was a real treat every time I would receive a new piece of equipment. I would try it out in our living room and dream about being out on the AT. Among other things, I got a new single wall tent and a lighter and warmer sleeping bag. I also changed to a different water filtration system. I started selling some of my older equipment to help offset the cost of the new gear.

I also joined a few groups on social media and started looking for advice from folks who had done the journey before. I listened to as many podcasts as I could. I was always listening as I was training. I also read about shelters, hostels, and anything I could learn about the various parks I would have to go through. Another concern I had were venomous snakes. Since we do not have any in Canada, I wanted to learn as much as I could, so I would be prepared.

Although I was concerned about snakes, my biggest concern was my arthritis. I wanted to complete the trail but not if it would cause long term issues with my health. I take a weekly injection that has to be kept refrigerated. My rheumatologist contacted the pharmaceutical company and found out the drug needed to be refrigerated to extend the life of the medication, but it could stay at room temperature for up to sixty days before it would deteriorate. So I was good for at least two months on the trail, and I figured since the first month would be cold enough, I could bring ninety days' worth of supplies. Being Canadian, I cannot ship drugs across the border, so I had planned to come home in ninety days to pick up my drug and then return to my hike. That's why I decided to start in the south and go northbound. That way instead of starting late May, I could start in the middle of March.

Before I stared, I was invited to give a talk about my upcoming hike at Abbey Landry School, a local school in Memramcook. Students from grade 7 and grade 8 attended the presentation. They had many interesting questions, and it was fun for me to talk to them and see the reactions on their faces. It's also amazing how youth see things differently than adults. I suggested I would send a daily update when I had phone reception and they could follow me all the way. They were very excited and for me it was one more incentive to complete the trail. I created a Facebook page just for my hike. Many folks told me that way they could live their dream through me. As far as I was concerned, the connection through Facebook was yet another way to keep motivated during rough times on the trail. I was determined I would not want to let my followers down.

The biggest concern people had was that I was going to get lost in the woods or be eaten by a bear. Some were also concern about venomous snakes and cougars. So many people asked me if I was taking a gun with me to protect myself. My cousin who I go alpine skiing with every year asked me if he could have my new set of skis if a bear was to kill me. I knew he was only kidding about the skis, but he was genuinely concerned he would lose his ski partner. I had seen many bears in the woods before, and they were always more afraid of me than I was of them. Snakes, however, were a real concern of mine since I had never seen poisonous snakes in nature before. Most of the people I talked to were skeptical that I was going to complete the long hike.

I started training in early December, 2017 more specifically to what I would be doing on the trail. I was already training six or seven days a week, but now the focus was more on hiking. Almost every day I'd walk in the woods with a light pack, and I always searched for hilly terrain. I did not have the luxury of any mountains close by so any hills I could find would have to do. I increased my pack weight and distance weekly. When the snow hit, I switch from hiking to snowshoeing. The preparation was so much fun since I got to spend hours outdoors in the forest. It was like I was already starting a new therapy. Knowing that one of the most challenging aspects of the hike is to keep the feet healthy, I also treated my feet three to four times a week with tincture of benzoin to try to harden the sole. I also switched to zero drop shoes, a shoe where the heel is the same height as the ball of the foot and started walking as much as I could barefoot in the house. I tried different types of socks and tried to double up on socks like so many do. That did not work for me, so I settled on as single pair of merino wool socks.

The doctor checked me out and said I was physically fit for the hike, but she recommended I get a tetanus shot and vaccine against rabies. She also gave me a prescription for a couple doses of antibiotics in case I got infected by a tick. Getting Lyme disease was a big concern. Another big concern was hypothermia. I had treated a patient once during an emergency call that was hypothermic and went into respiratory arrest. I was able to bring him back with assisted ventilation, but I knew hypothermia was a real threat that could kill me. I also paid a visit to my dentist to make sure all my teeth were healthy. He was concerned, however, about my bridge that was loose. He recommended I get the teeth pulled, but I decided I would take a chance that it would hold to the end.

I definitely did not want to cause any long-term harm to my health by being deprived from a healthy diet, so I looked for advice from a sport dietitian on ways to prepare my body before the hike and advice on nutrition in the back country. My plan was to put on some weight because I knew I was going to lose some. Instead she advised me that it would probably be better to keep a healthy weight and carry a bit more food and keep my calorie intake up. That sounded like good advice since the total weight on my knees would be less if I was lighter. I usually eat healthy and don't need to supplement my diet, but since I was going to be low on nutrients, she recommended I start with a multi vitamin for males over fifty and supplement with iron after my blood test showed I was borderline iron deficient. I got enough medications and supplements to last for six months. I also took out a medical insurance policy in case I would get hurt on the trail.

Plans were well on the way. Nat was working as an emergency health care nurse in a remote community in northern British Columbia and had a couple of weeks' vacation in March, so she planned on joining me for eight days at the start of my hike. My daughter had a friend in Atlanta and asked if she could put us up for the night and drive us to the trailhead. The friend was away at the time but said we were welcome to use her house, so I booked my flight for March to Atlanta and reserved a shuttle for us to get from the car rental place to Springer Mountain, the southern terminus.

Two weeks before I was due to leave for Atlanta, Lucille's mother was rushed to the cardiac unit with a serious heart problem. The next day my mom was also brought to the hospital by ambulance. So both my mother and mother in-law were in the hospital at the same time, and my departure was in jeopardy. It turned out my mother had a problem in her ears causing severe vertigo and was release a few days later. As for Lucille's mother, things got better after they told her they could probably fix the problem with stents. Her heart was only functioning at 25 percent, but the stent did bring her back up. She was released about a week later and before she knew it, she was feeling better than before she had the episode. My mother still did not approve of me leaving; but my wife was fine with me going, so I was on my way.

Chapter 7

With Nat

Ihad landed in Atlanta on the afternoon of March 21, 2018, and got a car rental. Then I went to the phone store to get a US sim card for my phone. I did some grocery shopping to get ready for the next morning. I was alone in a house that Nat's friend had loaned us. I called the shuttle driver to confirm he was picking me up at the car rental place and drive us to the trailhead. He told me he was booked and had no record holding a place for me. The trip was not starting well. I found out even before starting my hike that any plans when hiking the AT tend to fail. After emailing the driver the receipt he suddenly remembered. He claimed his phone had failed, and he had lost a lot of appointments. He said that he thought he recovered them all but must have missed mine. He finally agreed to pick me up later in the morning and drive me to the trailhead.

As I was lying in bed on March 21, 2018, I was completely overwhelmed with emotions. I was very excited to finally get to Georgia to start the trail in the morning. I was also glad that I was going to see Nat in the morning. I had not seen her in a few months. But I was also sad that I would not see Lucille or my other children and grandchildren for the next four or five months. I knew that hiking the AT would push me far outside my comfort zone, and I was also afraid it would push me too far. I had already been tested by staying in a home owned by complete strangers that night. I was worried that my shuttle driver would not show up in the morning as planned. I was scared that I would not be able to find Nat in the airport. Knowing that only about 10 percent of thru hikers actually complete the journey had me on edge. I was terrified that something would go wrong on the trail and that I may never return home. With all these and so many other thoughts and emotions going through my head; I hardly slept that night.

I picked up Nat up at the airport that morning at 5 a.m.; she had taken an overnight flight from Vancouver. I was afraid I would never find her in the Atlanta airport since it is the busiest airport in the world, and I was not familiar with it. All went well, though, and we were able to connect quickly. I took her back to the house so she could get a couple hours of sleep before heading out to meet the shuttle driver and drop the car at rental place. We stopped by an outfitter and a grocery store to gather the few items she needed to get for the trail. We also got a good last meal before heading out into the wilderness.

The shuttle driver called and said he would be about an hour late. He said his previous client's flight was late, but I suspected he was lying because he was overbooked and trying to fit everybody in. There was nothing I could do about it. He was a strange character to say the least. I finally understood why his booking was messed up when I saw him operate after we were in the van. He had a GPS on one side and his cell phone on the other side and was booking appointments as he was driving. It was an interesting ride to the trailhead. We picked up another hiker at Amicalolas Falls that was planning to do the whole trail. He was way out of shape and terrified. He told us he wanted to get away from his life as a farmer for a few months to clear his head. Later, I was kind of sorry I did not get his contact information because I never saw him again and wondered if he ever completed the trail.

We got to the trail head at 3 p.m. Nat was suffering from a bad cold and a headache; she only slept a few hours in the past two days. She later told me that she had never seen me so unfocused and worried than that morning. She said I could not even think straight; and she was right. I was on edge. We summited Springer Mountain, where the trail starts and then had to come back down. We made it to the first campsite and decided to set up for the night. We forgot to buy a lighter since we did not want to carry one on the plane. I asked a few hikers I met to see if they had an extra one I could buy. Finally we found a hiker who had two lighters and gladly parted with one. He told us to forward the goodwill along the way. They say that the trail provides, and it did, which was great because then Nat could have coffee and a warm breakfast the next morning. I was finally on my way to hike the AT after all the waiting and planning.

The campsite where we spent our first night still had a few tent spots, so we did not have any problem. It was quite cold that first night, but since I was tired, I slept relatively well. I was up quite early the next morning but decided to let Nat sleep since she was sick. By 9 a.m., I had not heard a peep from her and was concerned because the night had been cold. I woke her up to check up on her. She was feeling somewhat better, but her cold was still bad.

We had a quick breakfast, and she had her coffee before we set off for the day. It was a rainy morning and getting windy, and the air was still cold. That day we met quite a few hikers who had started their thru hike the day before and some had been at it already for a couple days. There was one guy who hiked with us for couple of nights. I am not sure if he was afraid to sleep alone or if he was getting fond of my daughter, but he seemed to want to tag along. He is another one I would have liked to have kept in touch to find out if he finished the trail. What I discovered early on is that the trail mostly runs on the side of the mountain ridges, and it's hard to find a flat spot.

You have to set up in gaps between the mountains where there is usually a big wind tunnel. So we had to start planning for ours sites for the night a bit better.

The second night Nat got a bad stomach issue and it came out the wrong end. She said she did not have enough toilet paper, so she had to crawl back to her tent to get some more. Fortunately, we were the only two tents around since we had set up camp away from the designated campsite. That next morning I let her sleep as long as she needed. She was feeling much better that day. It rained every day for the first five days we were together. It was also very cold and windy. One day at lunchtime it was so cold that we had to eat at a shelter where they had a fire going, so we could stay warm. Because it was so cold, whenever we weren't hiking, we had to take refuge in our sleeping bags. Nat's sleeping bag was not rated cold enough to stand the freezing nights, and she was miserable the first two nights, so after that second night we stopped at an outfitter on the trail where she bought a bag rated to fifteen degrees Fahrenheit. It was very expensive, but she really needed it.

On the third night, we tried to get to a certain campsite, but it was getting dark too fast. So with a friend we had met we set up our tents in an open pit next to a road crossing. The fourth night on the trail together there were many tents where we stayed. There was a family with five children who were also camping there. On the fifth night were going to hike into a nearby town to shower and resupply but could not make it because Nat was limping quite badly. So we had to set up in a gap between the mountains. At the time we tried to avoid shelters because my daughter was concerned about germs.

The terrain was really challenging in that stretch, but since I had trained a lot with weight in my backpack, I was okay. I took the approach early on to fix all the small problems before they get big. That paid out big as my hike progressed; but at the time I was not aware how much Nat was struggling till she started limping. She told me she had issues; however she insisted she was okay to push forward. We got trail magic a couple of times that day. One time a couple of guys in a pickup were giving out chips and pop. At another crossing some section hikers were handing out fresh fruits and candies before they headed out on the trail.

We got a shuttle into Helen, Georgia, and booked a hotel, so we could shower and resupply. It was our first day off the trail since we had started. After five days Nat was hurting too much with her shin splints, so she decided to call it quits. She was also suffering from blisters and hip issues. Her cold was getting better, but she was limping badly. She was concerned that it would cause permanent damage, so we decided the next morning she would head back to Atlanta and spend the rest of her vacation with a friend. She didn't get as far as she hoped, but still we had lot of fun and laughs despite all the issues. We had a great meal at a restaurant that evening. Since I had no reception in the mountains, it was also nice to be able to talk to my wife for the first time since I had started on the trail.

It was with a sad heart that I had to say goodbye to my daughter the next morning when the shuttle took me back to the trail. Despite all her ailments she still had enjoyed the hike a lot and had a great time. Her friend's husband picked her up later that day and took her back to Atlanta. I was very grateful to be able to hike a portion of the trail with Nat and knew I was going to miss her company, but now I was on my own for the first time.

Chapter 8

Finally on My Own

Now on my own it felt like a new start to the journey. It was also the first day it felt like spring. The sun was out all day, and I mistakenly thought winter was finally over. The terrain was very challenging, but the biggest problem in the early days was the weather. As I walked over the mountains, the trail snaked from one side of the ridge to the next. I was either sheltered from the wind and in the sun on one side or in the shade or battered by heavy wind on the other. The temperature changed twenty degrees from side to side.

Being alone also meant I would no longer have any hot meals while on the trail. Nat had brought a stove, but I decided before the hike that I would go stoveless, which meant I ate all my food cold. Very few thru hikers opted to go stoveless because they liked a warm cup of coffee in the morning. For me that was not an issue since I don't drink coffee. I went stoveless for convenience. I didn't want to have to carry fuel or water for cooking, and I didn't want to have to bother with cleaning dishes. Meals were usually quick because they really were just big snacks.

On the AT there are shelters called lean-tos every ten to twelve miles. They have three sides and a roof with the front side exposed to the weather. There are usually flat spots around the shelters to set up tents. That's where most hikers gather at the end of the day to enjoy socializing with other hikers. At the beginning the shelters were very crowded. After a few bad experiences, I decided to avoid the shelters. I would usually hike quite late into the day. When I got to one shelter all the good tent spots were taken. It was getting dark and too late to keep going, so I had to set up in a very uneven site. All night I kept sliding against the side of the tent and falling off my mattress. Another problem I had at some of the early shelters was that a lot of people were there to party not hike. I called them wannabe hikers. They stayed up late and were noisy. There was a lot of booze and drugs, but those hikers didn't last long on the trail.

The shelters were also usually infested with mice. With everybody eating at the same location and dropping food, the crumbs attract bears and mice. One night a mouse was trying to get into my tent. It was climbing on the mesh. I would snap at it to go away, but it kept coming back trying to get at my food. Normally when you are hiking, experts recommend you hang your food in the trees so that bears cannot get to it. And they say you never should eat in your tent. At the start of my hike it was too cold to eat outside, so I would eat in my tent all the time. I also get hungry in the middle of the night, so I had snacks close by. Besides bears are afraid of human, I thought, so unless they are tame they would avoid trying to get my food in my tent. So after a while I needed to get to sleep, and the only way I could keep that rodent away was to keep my head lamp on all night. Needless to say my lamp was dead in the morning, but the mouse had not chewed through my tent.

One cold morning I was feeling kind of low when I met this young guy in his early twenties. He was walking barefoot. He was not doing a thru hike, but he was doing twenty miles with no shoes. He had a great smile and was very friendly. His smile was contagious and the fact he was barefoot made my day. Sometimes it's the little things in life that can bring sunshine in somebody's heart. Early on, I was very happy hiking until it was time to go in town to resupply. Hiking on the trail was fun, but I disliked walking on the road. Strange as it may seem, I do not like walking at all. For some reason hiking in nature is different. A lot of hikers would hitchhike into town, but that stressed me out. I would always try to get a hotel that had a shuttle. For me going into town to restock was the most challenging part of the hike, even worse than the bad weather. The trail was rugged and hard, but it was simple and I enjoyed it.

On March 28, 2017, I crossed into North Carolina from Georgia. It was a milestone for me, and it felt good to have completed one state. Just a couple days later I reached the hundred mile marker, another milestone. I was hiking longer every day and loving every minute, even the hard days. I met a lot of friendly hikers but would only see them for a day or so as I was faster than most.

Nantahala Outdoor Center (NOC) is an outfitting company where you can rent rafts to go white water rafting. They are also right on the trail. I bought supplies and got my permit to enter the Great Smoky Mountain Park. They didn't allow backpacks in the store. I was scared leaving my pack outside, but a few hikers on the porch said they would watch it for me. After getting what I needed, I sat on the porch charging my phone and stuffing my face with food. I was able to talk to my wife without worrying about my batteries. It was a great afternoon, chatting with other hikers who were taking a couple of days off, or zeros as we called them, to rest and nurse some injuries. They told me there were extra spots where they were stealth camping just outside the village and asked me to stay. It was a warm day, the sun was out, and I got lazy. I spent way too much time with them before heading out. Leaving the NOC was one of my toughest climbs since the beginning because my pack was full of food, and it was late in the afternoon. The climb ~·· is over five thousand feet in elevation so when I finally set up my tent that night, I was beat but felt great and very happy.

A few nights later, I met a girl training to hike the Continental Divide that stretches from Mexico into Canada. She had done the AT a couple of years prior, so I was able to get great advice. Now that I had a little bit of experience, I could ask pertinent questions about the trail ahead. The next morning she only hiked for a little while because she was meeting a friend to do trail magic later in the afternoon. I enjoyed the morning as it was the first day that I hiked with somebody since Nat had left.

Spring was in the air. A few days later I started to see flowers; however, there were no leaves or even buds on the trees. A few birds were starting to sing, but the only wildlife I had seen so far were squirrels and mice. The nights were still very cold though. April 16, Easter Sunday, I headed into Robbinsville, North Carolina, for supplies. It was my first stop in a town since I was alone, and it was a new experience. When I hit Stecoah Gap, there was a shuttle driver picking up a girl to go into town. I offered to split the fair if I could get a ride too. I had already made hotel reservation at the San-Ran Motel. It was not a great motel, but it was close to the grocery store. And had laundry facilities, everything I needed. It was nice to be able to call my wife and the rest of family on Easter. I was also able to text Nat for the first time since she had left.

Her shin splint was getting better, and she was enjoying Atlanta. My grandson was missing me a lot, so I called my other daughter and also talked to him. I was able to update my log, shower, and wash my clothes. I also cleaned and dried all my gear. I ate a whole chicken and quite a bit more food. It turned out to be a great stop.

The next day I had to figure out how to get back to the trail, which was eleven miles away. I asked the motel operator, and she said it was not a big problem to hitch a ride to the trailhead. I should have hired a shuttle, but I wanted to get my first experience hitchhiking alone. After over two hours and four miles I was about ready to quit hitchhiking and just walk the rest to the trailhead. Then a nice older man finally picked me up. The traffic was fast. It was a dangerous section to hitchhike, and so many cars had gone by. I was very grateful to finally get picked up. He said he never goes by a hiker without picking him up. He wished he had the courage to hike the trail, but he was not brave enough, so he contributed by driving hikers whenever he saw one on the road.

That next day I was feeling homesick because I had talked with my family the day before. At midday I ate my lunch with a Swedish girl. I normally just talked about general stuff, but that day I needed to talk to someone. She reminded me of my daughters and was a good listener, so I opened up to her and told her I was homesick. Just being able to have someone listen to me made things a whole lot better. I thanked her for listening, and in the afternoon, I was okay again. Whenever I got to the top of a mountain I usually had phone reception, so I would call my family or send them a picture and a brief comment how I was doing. The views were incredible on sunny days.

On April 2, I reached Fontana Dam just before the start of the Smokies. It was early in the afternoon, and I decide to take the rest of the day off and rest a bit. I was about to get into the Smokies and was concern about all the regulations there. The Swedish girl finally showed up and her right ankle was hurting, so she decided to take a few zeros at the dam. I never saw her again after that day, but she'll probably never know how much she helped me. Fontana Dam is one of the common places that a lot of hikers quit before getting into the Smokies. There was a huge tent area with lots of partying. Most hikers were taking a zero. Some were meeting friends or family for the first time since they had started the journey. On the AT almost everybody uses a trail name instead of their real name. I met Ducky that day, and we became good friends and kept running into each other quite a bit. He was a pleasant young man that had also done an Ironman, so we had the AT and an Ironman in common. He was also funny and always had a big smile.

One big concern that I had was blisters. With all the rain that we got early on I worried I'd mess my feet up. But I had managed so far by taping or drying my feet as much as needed. I always tried to address any hotspots before they got too bad.

Chapter 9
The Smokies

As soon as I walked into the park, I encountered a park ranger. He informed me there was a lot of bear activity at the first shelter, so they had to close it. Some folks had gone hiking and left their food in the tent. While they were away a bear ripped through the tent trying to get the food. The ranger advised me never to leave my pack unattended since bears associate a backpack with food. There is a big problem with bears in the Smokies since there is no hunting there, and the bears are used to humans.

The park has strict rules about camping. Tenting is not allowed anywhere except in shelters area and only if the shelters are full—but a permit is required. I bought a backcountry camping permit back at NOC's. Thru hikers cannot reserve a slot in the shelters but section hikers can. So if hikers show up with a reservation and the shelter is full, the last thru hiker in the shelter has to give up his or her spot even if it's late in the evening and set up tent next to the shelter.

The first shelter I stayed in on the trip had two levels. There was a big tarp covering the open front to try to keep the cold wind from penetrating. It did help some, but there were cracks all over. I always have to relieve myself at night, so I slept on the second level close to the stairs. I met a nice couple, Stretch and Rambo Juice. They were experienced hikers and had done over twelve hundred miles on the Pacific Crest Trail the previous year. To my surprise it was also their first experience in a shelter too, and they were nervous. I was afraid to be in the way and bother people and had no clue how to behave in a shelter.

Pete with the Red Hair, a hiker I met in the Smokies also stayed with us that night and ended up hiking with me on and off for the next week. He was a nice young man in his mid-twenties. There are cable systems to hang the food bags so the bears cannot get them. That was good for my food, but it also meant I could not have my regular snack in the middle of the night. I knew I was going to wake up in the middle of the night hungry. Pete showed me how simple it was to use the cables. I did not wake up hungry since I did not sleep very well. One hiker was passing out ear plugs in the evening because he snored a lot. Turns out he had sleep apnea and kept everybody awake all night. I expected any minute I was going to have to perform CPR because he would stop breathing. My first night in a shelter was in the books, but I much preferred sleeping alone in my tent than with a bunch of strangers. Inside my tent, I felt like I was king in my castle.

At that time it was spring break in Tennessee, so the shelters were busier than usual. At that shelter three local hikers, a surgeon, his son, and his brother, who was also a medical doctor, spent the night with us. They had so many questions about thru hiking and were watching everything we did to try to learn. All three were obese and were doing a spring hike every year to try to stay fit and clear their minds. The surgeon was in his mid-fifties and told me he was going to get in shape after he had put his son through college. I encouraged him to start getting in shape now and spend more weekends in nature and not wait till it was too late. He said he worked over sixty hours a week and was saving for later in life, but clearly he was not considering his health in the plan. The next morning he told me he thought about our conversation and was going to invest into his health right away. I am not sure if he ever did.

Even though the scenery was spectacular, I wanted to get through the park as fast as I could because I did not like all the rules.

The following day, I met a hiker who was struggling. It was getting quite late in the afternoon, and he was just wearing a shirt and was shivering badly. I knew he was hypothermic. He was also very tired. I tried to help him, but he refused any assistance. He did not want to put on his jacket because he said it made him sweat too much. He was fairly overweight and even though I insisted he assured me he was fine. It took me forty-five minutes to get to the shelter. Fifteen minutes later there was still no sign of him. We were organizing a search party to go look for him when he stumbled into the shelter. He was in bad shape.

There was a fireplace in that shelter and the entrance was covered with a big tarp. Some hikers decided to try and get a fire going in the fireplace to warm him up, but it had rained all day and no matter how hard they tried they could not get it going. Everything was so wet, they even tried to use toilet paper soaked in Vaseline. They tried to use the stove canister fuel but nothing worked. At the end they gave up, and we did not get a fire going. The poor guy eventually warmed up in his sleeping bag. He said he was quitting his hike in the morning and taking the shortest way into town. That second night in a shelter was not much better than the first night. At least we did not have the sleep apnea hiker, but I did not sleep much better. I was still nervous sleeping with a bunch of strangers. Usually, I put my medication, cell phone, charger, and water filter in my sleeping bag to protect them against the freezing temperatures. With the chaos of all the people, I forgot and left my water filter in the side pocket of my backpack. It froze, so the next morning I had to get off the trail and go into Gatlinburg to buy a new filter.

Pete with the Red Hair told me that there was a church group doing trail magic at the Newfound Gap crossing. He said they were shuttling hikers into town at 10 a.m. and then back to the trail at 11 a.m. It was awesome to know I had a ride into town, and they had so much food. After I ate, about twelve of us headed into town in the van. I hurried to buy a new filter at the NOC store in Gatlinburg and topped off my food supply. I was disappointed when I found out the van had left about twenty minutes before and were not coming back to get us. Since I had to hitch back to the trailhead, I decided I may as well have a good meal in town. Seth, a friend who had also missed the van, and I hitched back to the trailhead together. After hitching for about thirty minutes we got a ride with a Russian girl who was going to visit the park for the afternoon.

After spending three nights in the Smokies I heard there was a cold front coming with snow in the forecast. I got to Standing Bear Hostel around noon; it had rained all morning and was already getting below freezing. That hostel has a good reputation on the AT. With the storm coming I figured it was a good night to have my first experience in a hostel. The bunkroom housed fourteen beds and by four in the afternoon every bed was taken. All the other sleeping areas were also full. Folks were setting up tents on the front porch of the house. I had to wait forever to use the tub where we did laundry by hand on a washboard. At least I was going to stay dry, and hopefully warm, for the night. Spending that night at that hostel was an experienced for sure. One hiker was paying for his hike by offering tattoos along the way. He was doing tattoos on the kitchen table in the dining room while hikers were eating. I figured I would eat in the bunkhouse. The staff were great though and very open and friendly. The store had an honor system. You kept track of what you purchased and paid when you left the hostel in the morning. The only thing that they kept locked up was the beer.

When I came back from showering I noticed that I had lost my wallet. I had that bad feeling in the stomach, knowing I had not paid enough attention to what I was doing. I went back and could not find it in the shower area. I asked the owner if somebody returned it. After I got back to my bunk it was on my bed with all my money in it. Nobody had touched it. I must have overlooked it, but it was a warning to be more careful with my stuff even though most hikers can be trusted. That night we got a few inches of snow, and it was very cold and windy. When I had called for a reservation, the hostel told me they didn't take reservations but never turned anybody away. That night, however, they were so full, they had to turn hikers away. They would allow tents on their property, but they still had to pay and sleep on a lawn. Hikers were better off sleeping in the forest where there was shelter from the wind.

The next morning, I left before daylight to get in a good day of hiking since I had hiked only half the day before. There was only one set of footprints in the snow before me as another hiker had left even earlier than I did. I figured I would get breakfast on the trail when the sun came up. I was just wearing running shoes, so I was glad somebody made tracks before me. It was one of the nicest sunrises I saw on the trail with the rays coming through the white branches loaded with fresh snow. The wind was calm, and the trees were so beautiful. Everything was white for miles. At lunch we were surprised at a road crossing. A couple of trail angel families had set up a stand and offered hot homemade vegetable soup, stew, fruits, soft drinks, and candy bars. They had a two-year-old girl with them with such a warm smile, she reminded me of my grandchildren. It was another memorable day.

I was happy when I got to Hot Springs, North Carolina, a very nice trail town. I met Red Hair Pete and a few other hikers at a restaurant. We ate so much food. I got a room at Elmer's Sunnybank Inn where I had shipped a new pair of shoes before I left home. It felt so good to get a hot shower and sleep in a warm bed in my own room after having frozen my butt off for a week. Deluxe, another friend and a very experienced hiker, was also spending the night there. We had a great conversation late into the evening about previous hikes he had done. We kept in touch for a few weeks after that night, running into each other from time to time. Hot Springs was a great town to resupply as the trail goes right through it. I felt rested and rejuvenated after an afternoon off and a good night in a clean bed in a private room. I survived the Great Smoky Mountains. I had slept in shelters, hostel, and experienced snow. I was now broken in. Other than spending nights awake in the shelters and freezing my butt off, the Smokies had actually been fun.

Chapter 10
Virginia

I left Hot Springs at early light in order to do a good day of hiking with my new pair of sneakers. I had a full stomach and was well rested. Most of the hikers I had met in town were taking a day off. The weather was getting warmer, and I was still having fun. By then I was averaging around twenty miles a day. I met a group of younger hikers on Bald Mountain that I had never seen before. I called them the Group of Seven. From then on, I kept bumping into them at lunchtime or at water sources, and we eventually became good friends.

The week I left Hot Springs, North Carolina, I had accomplished nearly four hundred miles. After an extremely hot day, where I almost got dehydrated, the weather turned, and I got hit by heavy rain for the next three days. On the third day the forecast was calling for hundred-mile-per-hour winds, and it was freezing in the evening. I had been on the trail almost a month, and even though it had looked like spring was coming, here we were getting blasted with cold again. I had been determined to stay away from shelters after the Smokies, but that night, I had to get away from the weather. I managed to reach a barn that had been converted into a shelter around two in the afternoon. I figured I would eat, get warm, and then continue on, but Deluxe convinced me to stay. It was a wise decision. That night over twenty-five hikers crammed in the Overmountain Shelter. The first level was open to the elements, but the second level was boarded. The snow was blowing so hard we had to put our tent covers up to plug the cracks between the boards.

It got very cold that night, and in the morning everything was frozen. Some folks were trying to melt their shoe laces with their stoves so they could put them on their feet. I had opened my shoelaces from my shoes in the evening so I was okay. With the storm blowing the next day many folks were going to stay put. Some of the hikers had made reservation in the next town, so they had to move on. The Group of Seven had made reservations earlier that week but told me that the hostel where they were staying was full. I tried to book a room in town but could not. Two girls in the group, Bake Oven and Sprout, told me that if I could not get a room when I got in town, they would let me stay on the floor in their private bedroom, so I figured I would push to town with them.

Eleven, another girl that had spent the night with us in the shelter, couldn't get her frozen shoes on her feet, so she decided to hike nine miles into town in crocks. The wind was so strong and pushing us all over the place. Going through the bald mountains in the blizzard, Eleven got disoriented and I met her going in the wrong direction. I told her to follow me, even though I wasn't sure I was going the right way either. Everything was covered with snow, and we were above the tree line, so we could not see any blaze and were not sure where we were heading. We were just following another set of tracks in the snow and hoped they were going to the right way. After going over a few summits I finally got into town. It was going to get even colder that night, so I was fortunate to get a room in the hostel with the two young girls. One of them was from France so we were able to have a discussion in our native tongue.

Some folks just try to make other people miserable. It is rare on the trail since most hikers try to help each other. But that night in the hostel a lady around my age complained when one of the younger hikers turned the TV on to watch a hockey game. She said he was being rude and turned to me for support. She wanted him to go watch the game in the uninsulated kitchen where it was very cold. He also looked to me for a cue about what he should do. I told her if she did not like the game, she should just not watch it. She did not like my answer, but all the younger guys and gals smiled in approval. That night they played games and drank beer as I enjoyed the warmth. I had been so cold for the past few days, it felt good just hanging around with friends.

After that nasty storm we got only one more day with a little dusting of snow. The warmer weather was finally coming. The locals told us it was one of the coldest springs they ever had. After zigzagging between North Carolina and Tennessee for a while, I finally made it into Virginia, the state with most trail miles. It was April 19, 2017, and I was feeling blessed; I now had my trail legs and had been able to avoid blisters even though we had more days of wet weather than sunny days. It had been over a month since I had left Springer Mountain. I was enjoying myself so much, and I was in great spirits. I was thinking everybody should experience the trail as I was experiencing it. Life was great even though I was missing my family at home.

By this point most of the partiers on the trail had dwindled to just a few. Most hikers that made it to mile five hundred were real hikers and were serious about accomplishing the journey. I realized how fortunate I was to be able to be part of that group knowing that just a few years before I was almost crippled with arthritis and alcohol. Everybody was so helpful to each other, and the trail angels were helpful in so many ways. Crossing the road one day, I was not too sure where I was because the app on my phone was not working and I could not get my bearings. I was trying to get it to work when a lady in her eighties stopped and asked me where I wanted to go. I told her I was looking for the post office in town. I needed to get a new pair of shoes that Altra had sent me. She had very little room in the car because it was loaded with stuff from her church, but she managed to squeeze me in and drive me to the post office.

In the middle of Virginia my tent started leaking in the heavy rain. I also needed a new air mattress since my old one had been patched so many times. One cloudy day, as I was coming to a road crossing, I hoped for some trail magic. I was feeling low and needed a boost. I sat by the road with nobody in sight and suddenly a bird flew by and shit on my head. It was sad, but I could not help but laugh. And strangely enough it cheered me up. Reaching town always reminded me of the westerns I'd watch when I was young. A cowboy would reach town and head for the saloons for a warm bath, liquor, and food. To be able to get a hot bath and warm food into my belly was a real treat. I knew I could not go for liquor, however, since that would quickly put an end to my hike.

During my hike I discovered that I could outwalk spring. Since I was doing about a hundred miles every four days and heading north, I had outpaced spring three times. I had seen all the leaves come out and seen everything turn green, but then I hiked fast enough going north to be back where everything was still gray and the trees were just budding. The winter after I decided to hike the trail, I read the book *"Walking with Spring"* by Earl Shaffer. He was the first man to complete a thru hike of the AT in 1948. A lot of hikers would hike listening to podcast or music with earbud in their ears. I had earphones but decide not to use them. Instead I listened to the sound of nature. The birdsongs were so wonderful on those sunny and warm days. The forest was alive. One day I saw a big snake which was blocking the trail. It was not moving out of the way, so I figured I would throw my hiking pole to scare it away. After about ten minutes, the snake finally and slowly moved off the trail.

Most of the hikers I had been hiking with had stopped for a couple days for rest and relaxation in Damascus, Virginia. I did not want to be tempted to have a drink, so I had kept on hiking. We kept in touch through social media, and I figured they would catch back up with me eventually since they were all younger than me, but by then I was averaging about twenty-five miles per day. I was passing a lot of hikers who had started much earlier than me almost every day. I would see them only once or for a day or so and then they were gone. For the most part I was hiking alone. Sometimes I would pass faster hikers when they would go into town and not see them for a few days and then they would pass me and so forth.

When I first got on the trail, I was in a great shape physically. At most I wanted to lose only about ten pounds. With the warmer weather and the increased mileage, I was starting to lose weight too fast, so I started drinking olive oil or avocado oil before every meal. It tasted awful, but it was what I had to do. My meals at that time consisted of dried fruits and dried oatmeal for breakfast. I would have a tuna sandwich for lunch and cheese sandwich for diner, along with an energy bar every two hours. I would also have about five servings of nuts and an energy bar before going to sleep. Having to carry out my garbage posed a problem in the warmer weather. After carrying an empty pouch of tuna during warm weather for five days, the smell in my backpack was getting unbearable, so I had to switch from tuna to almond butter and honey for my lunches. After it got warm, I would only eat tuna when I knew I was going to be crossing a road later that day that had a garbage can.

With the warmer weather also came more bear activity around the shelters. Hikers were chasing bears away from their food bags around the shelters. One night I thought a bear was inside my tent trying to steal my food. I could feel his breath on my neck. I looked for my hiking pole and yelled loudly to scare him. When I turned my light on, there were no bears anywhere. My tent had not been ripped as I thought. I had just had a vivid dream. I had the exact same dream the following night but did not yell even though it felt just as real. I turned my light on just to see that it was yet another dream.

I always enjoyed meeting volunteers working on the trail. With the warmer weather they were out working a lot more now than at the beginning. I would always take the time to talk with them. I always thanked them for their hard work. I was not just being nice; I truly appreciated the fact that people took time bettering the trail so that hikers like us could go out and enjoy it. Trail magic is so wonderful, but meeting and talking to people who maintained the trail always made my day. I have been a volunteer and understand why folks volunteer their personal time. Seeing them at work gave me joy.

At the beginning of my hike, if I cut or scratch myself, it would take forever to heal. Being always in a dirty environment it was really hard to keep a wound clean. A small scratch would take forever to heal. Later in the hike, even a bad cut would heal in about three days. My body had gotten accustom to the bacterial environment and the dirt. Nature has a wonderful way of working.

Chapter 11
Shenandoah

It was late April and the weather had finally warmed up considerably and I felt great. I could now hike wearing shorts and a short sleeved shirt during most of the days. One cooler morning I was wearing my jacket when I came upon a young couple. They were section hikers with a medium size dog that was not on a leach. He went by me and then suddenly turned around and bit my arm. I was able to pull my arm back but not before he cut through my skin and tore my jacket. I was so furious. I told that couple that the dogs should be on a leash and that they were irresponsible. They assured me they would keep him tied up and that he had never done this before. They offered a Band-Aid to fix my jacket, as if that would help. Later that day, faster hikers passed me, and I asked them if they saw a couple with a dog. They told me they did and the dog was still running loose. It was one of the few times that I was really upset during my hike.

News travel fast on the trail. There was a forest fire just before McAfee Knob, one of the iconic destinations for hikers. I was about three days south of the closed section. We were not sure how long it was going to stay closed. Some hikers were getting shuttled passed the fire and hiking back south to their jumping spot. Some were just skipping it while others were waiting it out in hostels. I was not sure what I was going to do when I got there. That was one of the sites I did not want to miss. The day before I got there, I misjudged my traveling distance. I had spent way too much time enjoying the view and warming up on Dragons Tooth, a popular overlook, and had not noticed the time flying by. I started coming down and it got dark quickly. I could not find a decent camping spot till I was all the way down to the bottom. I was traveling with just my headlamps when suddenly my batteries died. It was really dark, so I took my cell phone lamp and dug into my backpack where I had spare set of batteries. By the time I found a good tent site, I had hiked over two hours down a mountain in the dark.

The next morning luck followed me around. I left early and got to the next road crossing, where the trail was closed by the rangers on account of the fire, around ten. Vagabond Jack, a hiker whose podcast I had been following before I got on the trail was there. He had been forced to abandon his hike because of a hernia, but he had decided to do some trail magic before heading back home. He knew exactly what hikers craved and had great food to offer. To make things even better, I found out they had just reopened the trail that morning. It was a clear sunny day, and I could get some great pictures on top of McAfee. I would have stayed up on the knob longer since it was so nice, but I had to leave because I was getting sunburnt. After McAfee Knob came another spectacular view at Thinker Cliff. I did not learn my lesson from the previous day and spent too much time on Thinker Cliff. I had to come down in the dark again in what was considered one of the hardest sections of the hike so far. I guess I was getting too comfortable and confident with my hiking abilities because the forest fire closed the trail again for a few days. I started meeting many hikers I had not seen before.

Most of the hikers I met around that time were younger hikers who had started from Springer a few days before me and even back in February. I met a couple of young guys called Beach Bum and Irish. They had taken a year off after graduating high school. I also met a couple in their late twenties that had sold their house and decided to go hike for a living. We had diner at a campsite one night with a few new hikers I met that day. I could finally enjoy socializing by a campfire since it was now comfortable in the evening. I had enjoyed chatting with Rondo, a thru hiker I just met earlier in the week and a couple of his friends.They cooked a huge meal on the fire. They had potatoes, peppers, vegetables, and pepperoni all wrapped in tinfoil. He was missing his girlfriend and was excited she was going to meet him in Harpers Ferry. That night a young girl named Sunshine was also enjoying the fire. I was amazed at how many young hikers were on the trail and that even young girls were brave enough to hike alone. That evening I also treated my clothes with Permethrin for the second time since many hikers were starting to get ticks on them.

One evening I had enough food for about two days. There was a town about twelve miles off the trail the following day or the next town was sixty miles away. I came across a ridge runner and asked him for advice. Ridge runners are folks hired by the Appalachian Trail Conservancy to monitor the trail and make sure hikers follow the rules. He said it could be done. I figured if he thought I could do it I might as well go for it. One thing that he did not mention was that I would have to cross the Priest and Three Ridge Mountain. They are two very technical and very tough mountains. That day he also showed me an invasive plant called garlic mustard that is edible, so for a few weeks after that I could get some green right on the trail.

That first day I was able to go twenty seven miles, so I figured the next day I could push and do thirty-three. It was my wedding anniversary that day, and I felt quite lonely. I always missed my family a lot more on special days. Unfortunately the next day I only hiked twenty-three miles and ate my last bit of food before going to bed. The following morning I had to get up and hike ten miles on an empty stomach before reaching the trailhead to hitchhike into Waynesboro, Virginia. I knew I was not going to die, but that was the first time I had completely run out of food since I had started. I was very hungry when I got in town around noon. I was always glad to get warm food as I got off the trail, but that day it was quite a bit more welcomed. What they called hiker hunger hit me hard that day. I just kept eating and then went back for more.

It was May 8, 2018, ten days since I had a shower or washed my clothes. I got to the hotel room and soaked for over an hour in warm bath filled with Epson salt. That was such a nice feeling. It is amazing how much we take a bath for granted in the so-called normal world. I spent the afternoon shopping for food and tent pegs that I had lost. For some reason I kept losing a tent peg every now and then. Sleeping in a warm clean bed that night felt good. The next morning I got a big breakfast before returning on my journey. Running out of food made me buy way too much food on this resupply. I was also not aware of all the restaurants and shops available in the Shenandoah Valley.

The Shenandoah National Park has been designated as wilderness preserve and is protected as part of the AT on the National Wilderness Preservation System. It is supposed to be preserved, but I was crossing the Skyline

Drive every few hours. There were so many motorcycles it sounded more like a city park than a national park. The only thing I liked about the park was that I could get food at restaurants and canteens along the way. I could also get showers at the campsite and get rid of garbage at almost every road crossing. The park had strict rules when it came to camping though. And I would always hang my food bag since there were lots of bears that were not afraid of humans.

Most hikers I talked to had seen several bears in the park. Every time I came to a campground or a picnic area, it always brought me back to when I was a young boy watching Yogi Bear on television. I pictured the park ranger fighting with Yogi who would steal the food basket. Whenever I saw tourists having lunch, I looked for a bear lurking. I made it through the park without seeing a single bear, but it brought back so many memories watching cartoons in my early years.

The trails in the park have a much better grade than further south, and thru hikers can usually get more distance in a day. The second day in the park I started to get shin splints. It was hurting more and more each day, so I had to cut my mileage to less than twenty miles per day. I ran into a nurse that was thru hiking, and she informed me that the only way to get rid of shin splints is to take a couple weeks off the trail with no hiking. I did not take any time off and managed to keep on going through the pain. On a ski trip in Alberta in 2017 I had met a couple from Virginia named George and Karen. I told them I was planning to hike the AT and they told me to call them when I passed the Shenandoah. They had a really nice ranch near Linden and I figured that would be a good time to take a bit of rest since I was injured.

Along with warmer weather came another challenge. We started having frequent violent thunderstorms. One day I was trying to get over a summit before the lightning got too close. I was about a hundred yards from the summit when a lightning bolt hit very close to me. I immediately dropped my hiking poles and sat down. I saw four more strikes just above me on the summit. I waited for a good twenty minutes after the storm had passed to proceed further. That day I also got hit by fairly big ice pellets along with heavy wind. That had been a close call, and with the heavy rain causing the trails to be wet and slippery. I could not get to where I wanted and had to sleep at a higher elevation than I would have preferred. I was soaked and had to set up camp before dark. I knew more of the storm was coming, and there would be strong winds that night. I always made sure that there were no loose branches above my tent that could fall, but that night I had to be extra careful.

It was out of character for me to call complete strangers and ask for help, but I wanted to push myself outside my comfort zone. And I needed a couple of easy days after the storm. I contacted George in the morning, and he picked me up at the trailhead. I had only hiked a couple miles that day, so I was not tired. I had been looking forward to spending a bit of time off the trail. After he picked me up, he kept putting his window down in the pickup and then closing it again. It was warm but not hot enough to ride with the window down. It later donned on me that it was my smell he was trying to avoid.

George and Karen were great hosts. They had such a nice, clean ranch where I had lunch and spent the afternoon relaxing. I even helped by cleaning out the horse trailer and watched as a couple farriers shoed a few horses. After I got a shower and washed my clothes, we had a nice dinner; barbeque chicken with lots of fresh vegetables. They had wine, but that part I had to decline. We chatted late into the evening on the front porch. It was a nice warm spring evening. They were excellent trail angels, and I got special kind of trail magic.

They told me I could stay at the ranch as long as I wanted until my leg healed. They said I could help around the barn if I wanted to or just stay and rest. I had asked them if they had horse medication that I could put on my shin splint. It worked wonders, and the next morning my leg was feeling much better. I had six eggs from their free-range chickens along with toast, fruits, and fruit juice. Then George took me on a ride in the truck and gave me a tour around the county. We stopped to get groceries and then he drove me back to the trailhead where I continued on my journey. Maybe I should have stayed there for a few days because we got hit with lots of rain that night. Karen had packed me a few apples to bring with me. Although they were too heavy to be carrying, I couldn't refuse her kindness. It was great when I met a young couple and was able to do some trail magic of my own and share my apples. The rain and wind kept coming for days.

Reaching the thousand-mile mark on May 17 gave me a great feeling of accomplishment, and anytime I conquered something grand, I always reflected back on how far I'd come since my days of drinking.

Chapter 12
Harpers Ferry

It rained for eight days straight. The ground was soaked, and the trail was like a brook. I met a couple of high school students who were out for a week on the trail as part of their outdoor education. They were scared and mentioned that they had just crossed a brook that was up to their hips. They complained that they had picked the wrong week for their adventure, but I assured them that this was how good memories were made. They kind of smiled and agreed they would have some good stories to tell when they got back in class. Brooks that we could normally rock hop were very challenging to ford. After I crossed the one that the two teens were talking about, I decided to set camp for the night.

The next morning the wind had picked up and the rain continued coming down, making it nine days in a row. A thru hiker I met the day before named Sour Croute caught up to me and told me the trail was closed just pass Harpers Ferry, the town we were going that day. He looked paranoid and scared, like he had seen a ghost. He told me that a few trees had fallen very close to him and almost killed him. There was a shelter ahead of us with a full-time keeper, and Sour Croute said he was going to stop there for the night or at least to get an update from the trail. I had not seen any danger so I suspected he must have smoked something good. I thought it was prudent to also stop at that shelter to get some news. The shelter, however, was half a mile off the trail and down a very steep hill. I was anxious to make it to Harpers Ferry and didn't want to hike an extra two miles, so I decided to push on.

The town of Harpers Ferry is known as the half way point on the AT, although it's not quite half way from Springer. My sister Liette was meeting me in Harpers Ferry the next day, and Lucille was coming with her to surprise me. I was not supposed to know my wife was accompanying her, but I had figured it out a while back during various conversations with the two of them. I had not mentioned anything because I didn't want to spoil their surprise. The wind was getting stronger and huge branches started falling close to me without any warning. One fell just about two feet in front of me. They call those big breaking branches widow makers. I could see why Sour Croute was scared. There were trees down across the trail at quite a few spots at that point.

He caught up with me later that afternoon around five. He was younger and a faster hiker than I was. He told me that the trail was officially closed past Harpers Ferry and that the ATC suggested hikers bypass all of Maryland. New York had also been hit very hard by the storm and recommended hikers bypass that state also. Even though I had known him for only a little while, we decided to share a hotel room Harper Ferry. I was soaked and all my gear was drenched. There was one campsite in town off the trail, but it was under water.

When we got to the hotel, it was double the price that we expected because it was a Friday night. We asked for a discount, but the lad said it was almost full and they did not give discounts on the weekend. While we were contemplating if we should take the room or not the manager walked in. We figured he was going to kick us out of the lobby since we were dirty and soaked and had not booked a room yet. Instead of telling us to leave, though, he asked us if we were in the military. We were not. He said they also had discount for state employees. I told him I was a volunteer firefighter and Sour Croute taught night school at a community college. He gave us a 60 percent discount, so we got the room right away. I was so happy because I just could not sleep on the street that night. I was so cold and wet, and I was in danger of hypothermia. Sour Croute told me he had been thrown out of the liquor store when they found out he was just there to warm up and not to buy liquor. They had told him he was bad for business.

While we were in the lobby, I had notice lady complaining to the manager that her room had not been cleaned. She was demanding another room and making a big fuss about it. To our surprise when she heard us talking about the trail closure, she told us she was going to section hike Maryland the next morning for a week. She said she was a marathon runner and that her friend could drive us past the closure if we would let her accompany us. She said normally she would be okay by herself and had planned to be alone, but after hearing about our day's experience she was scared to go alone. It was the first time she was going for an overnight hike, and while taking her along would have been the gentlemanly thing to do, after hearing her complain about a dirty room, we both figured it would be prudent not to have her hike with us. I usually like to help other hikers, but I was wary of taking her along. Besides, I was only hiking a few miles the next day and then was going to meet up with my sister.

After we checked in, we asked the manager if there was a good place to get food close by. It was already past eight. He said there was a store about two miles away that was still open, and he offered to drive us there and wait for us till we got some food. He said there was also a pizza place about five miles away, and they delivered. Once in the room I took my first shower in two weeks. I had been so cold that day, and the water felt so nice and warm; it was the best shower I got on the trail. We opted for both options for the food when the manager called us and said he was ready to go to the store. I got fried chicken, two yogurts, juice, and fruits. I did not buy anything for breakfast because the hotel had complimentary breakfast. When we got back, we ordered a large pizza to split. I could eat so much food and was still hungry.

Later that night I called my wife and chatted for a while. Before I hung up, I slipped and mentioned that I would see her the next day. That kind of spoiled her surprise, but I quickly changed subject. I had decided not to stay in a hotel or hostel after it had warmed up, but nine days straight of rain broke me. It was so wonderful sleeping in a warm bed instead of a wet tent and damp sleeping bag.

We had spread our gear all over the room the night before to dry. Checkout was at eleven, so we pushed it as late as we could in order to make sure everything had time to dry.

Harpers Ferry is a tourist town with lots of history. It's a very famous trail town. The ATC has a headquarter there. We were going to get our yearbook picture at the office and also to find out the status of the trail. There were so many hikers in town that Saturday waiting for the trail to reopen. It had been closed for a few days already and was going to be closed for another five days or so after the rain stopped. An ATC member said we just needed to skip three miles of trail that was under water, and we would still be considered official thru hikers since that was an official closure and the correct route was to by-pass.

Sour Croute was bummed that he had to skip three miles. He was what we call a purist and wanted to cover every inches of the trail. If he left the trail to go in town, when he got back to the trailhead, he would start back on the same side of the road that he had left. He was struggling hard with his options: stay put for five days or skip three miles of the trail. He was also hiking with a young couple he was meeting again the next day. For them skipping the three miles was not an issue so he finally decided to bypass the flooded trail. I had no issues skipping that section of trail since the by-pass was the official route and besides the trail changes every year by a few miles for one reason or another. The trail used to be around two thousand miles at one time.

That Saturday, May18, 2018, I did my shortest distance since I had started the journey. I hiked only two miles from the hotel to the bridge where the closure was and then backtracked to the ATC center to get my picture taken for the yearbook. I saw so many hikers I had not seen in quite a while. Almost every hiker stops to get their picture taken, visit the museum or meet friends and family. Being halfway on the trail it's a place where much reunion takes place. It's also a place where many hikers decide to call it quits. On the trail you can be just a couple hours apart and not see one another for weeks, but when everybody congregates in town, you meet people again. It was fun to share stories with fellow hikers that had done over a thousand miles like me. It was a major milestone.

Sour Croute and I went to lunch with other hikers and stuffed our faces again. I had told them that my sister would drive them to the other side of the flooded trail when she got there. Later that day I met my sister, but my wife was not with her in the camper. I was sad but figured she had dropped her off before she got to where we were supposed to meet. My sister was showing us the one room camper and said, "here is the bathroom." That was strange to show the bathroom to hikers, but actually my wife was hiding there. I was very happy to see her; it was one of the highlights of the trip.

Lucille and Liette were going to stay with me for five days. They would drop me off in the morning at the trailhead and pick me up again at a parking area further up the trail where I told them I would be. It was funny because almost every day they would get lost even though they had a GPS. I ate so much when I was with them. I also had the luxury to hike with a lighter pack since I only had to carry food and water for the day. That's what's called slack packing; it also gave me a good chance to recover from my shin splint injury. I also got a chance to treat my clothes with permethrin to protect against ticks. It is recommended to treat your clothes every four to six weeks and since the spray is heavy to carry, I normally wanted to do that while I was spending a night in town.

There was only one bed in the camper, so we shared the same bed. They thought it was a bit strange, but for me it was way more comfortable than sharing a shelter with complete strangers. During the day they would try to do trail magic to help other hikers. The five days went by so fast. It had been a great visit. I was sad to see them leave. For almost week after being with my wife and sister I was homesick. The first day I was sad, but then everyday it got better, and I adjusted back to the life of the trail.

I was just passed the halfway point and made the decision not to stay one more night in a hotel or hostel on my adventure.

Chapter 13

PA

I was being transformed into a different person without realizing it. I was getting way more confident with myself, maybe even too courageous. My attitude toward life, nature, and other people was changing. I was a lot more trusting with everybody. I was starting to really make peace with myself and starting to forgive myself for my sins of the past. It was like a new beginning; the world had not changed but I had. It's amazing how much you can appreciate the little things like getting a bottle of water or passing by a trash can on the side of the road where you can get rid of garbage. Water, toilet paper, food, and getting rid of garbage were the most important things for me at that time. I would not even look at the weather forecast since it didn't really matter. Every day I would get up in the morning, eat, and then hike. I had also learned never to have lunch before crossing a road because there may be trail magic at the road. Even though the journey was way beyond what I had expected and I was overwhelmed by the overall experience, trail magic always made my day better.

After Harpers Ferry the trail dynamics changed again. We started to see flip floppers or flippers as we called them. We were called NOBOs because we started at Springer and head north. Some hikers start their hike in Harpers Ferry and go either north or south to the end and then would come back to Harpers Ferry and go the other way to the other end. They flip-flopped their hike.

I caught up with Ducky after Harpers Ferry, and he was complaining about the flippers behavior at the shelters at night. They didn't use their red lamps at night and would blind him. They didn't have common sense with shelter etiquette. It was funny listening to him. It always made me laugh to think how we were now experienced hikers, and they should just be quiet. For the most part I enjoyed the flip floppers even though most of them were new to long distance hiking. They reminded me what I was like just over six weeks back. And now it seemed like an eternity since I had left Springer Mountain way back in Georgia.

Usually they would ask me for advice like I had done when I first started in March. After a couple of incidents I started to see why Ducky was complaining. I dropped into an outfitter in a nearby town to buy a new water filter. A flip flopper asked me why I was buying that particular brand. Before I could tell him my reason a girl who was hiking with him proceeded to tell him that she had done all her research. She told him that the filter I was getting had the best flow rate and great reviews, but she did not like it because it was not compatible with her water bottle. She went on and on for over ten minutes about which water filter to buy. She never gave me a chance to talk. After listening to her trying to justify why she got a different water filter, I gave up and headed to the grocery store. He never did find out why I preferred the filter I was buying.

One day at lunch I stopped to talk to a young flip flopper couple. The guy was having a bad time with his running shoes and was contemplating getting a pair of hiking boots. He asked my opinion about boots, but even before I could respond, he proceeded to tell me he had made up his mind that he was going to get a new pair in town. I personally preferred running shoes, but I was going to suggest he try hiking boot since he was having issues with his ankle and feet. I thought all was settled and we would move onto another subject but then he started to lecture me about why I also should try hiking boots. I had hiked over a one thousand miles in my shoes, but since he was trying boots, I guess he felt everybody should. It's amazing how much people try to rationalize and justify every decision they make. I tried to talk to all the flippers I could and get their views and feeling of the trail as they saw it. I had learned so much and had gained so much experience.

My attitude and mind-set had also changed after crossing that halfway mark. Before Harpers Ferry when I met someone on the trail and they asked me if I was going all the way, my answer always was, "that's the plan." After that halfway point when I was asked the same question, I would answer, "yes." I was way more confident that, barring any injury, I would finish. After Virginia, which holds a quarter of the trail alone, the states started to go by fast. I knew that two states coming up were going to be tough. I had heard so much about the rocks of Pennsylvania and the White Mountains in New Hampshire.

It was May 22, 2018; I had been on the trail for two months, the warmer weather meant the trail was also getting a lot busier with day and section hikers—especially on the weekends. I was always checking out the day hikers backpacks to see if they might have extra food. If they did, I would try to strike a conversation and many times was able to score some fruits or snacks. They wanted to hear all about my hike and in return I was looking for food. My view on life had changed. Before my hike I had a real hard time asking or accepting help from strangers. But now I could see that most people are genuine and want to help others while expecting nothing in return. There were so many wonderful experiences happening to me almost every day.

The rocks in Pennsylvania were not as bad as I expected in the first section. I had heard that the folks were not friendly in the Keystone state, but that was not my experience. I really liked the state from the start. Toward the end, however, the rocks really got to me. It was hard to find water on the trail and the weather was getting hot. There was a stretch for about twenty-nine miles without a water source, so I had to ration to make sure I had enough water to make it through. Some hikers would fill their stomach with as much water as they could to the point of nausea. I tried to stay hydrated for hours before I would get to a dry section rather than overhydrate at the last minute. With all the long-distance training I had done, I knew it was not good to overdo it. On that long stretch I got lucky. Ducky and Throw down were waiting for me at a road crossing to see if I wanted to join them for a beer in the tavern. I was not interested in a beer, but since they were going into town, they gave me the rest of their waters.

The rocks in Pennsylvania were really doing a number on my shoes so I ordered a pair to be shipped to the post office in Port Clinton. I was not aware the coming Monday was May 28, Memorial Day, so when I got in town early that morning the post office was closed. Even worse it didn't open until 2 p.m. on Tuesday, so I decided

I would tape my sneakers and have the post office forward my shoes to another post office further north.

The climb from Lehigh Gap was really tough. It was steep and very technical. It was the toughest section I had encountered thus far, but I still enjoyed the ascent. When I got to the top, since it was a warm and sunny day, I took advantage and stopped for a few hours to patch my leaking air mattress. It had about six holes in it, and I would wake up in the middle of the night on the cold ground. Later that day I saw a big black animal with a very long tail. I was not sure what it was, but to me it looked like a black panther. Later I talked to some local hikers, and they mentioned that some cougars had been sighted in the area, but they had never heard of a black one. I will never know what I saw fleeing that day, but I do know it was big and black and was not a bear. I am sure glad it did not want anything to do with me.

On the last day in Pennsylvania it was May 31, 2018, my birthday. I usually don't like to celebrate my birthdays, but I felt kind of lonely not having the children with me. It was after six in the evening, and I had not heard anything from home. I had turned on my phone at every summit, and nobody had sent me any text wishing me happy birthday. It was raining hard and had rained for a few days, so the rocks were very slippery. I fell four times that day got a bad cut on one of my legs. When I reached the last summit before Delaware Gap, I turned on my phone again and got a video call from my granddaughter signing me happy birthday. That really helped cheer me up till I got into town.

In town there was a place called Church of the Mountain Hiker Center run by a church group. It has a bunkhouse and couches where they offer hikers a free bed and shower. The bunkhouse was filled for the night, so I could not get a bed, but I preferred my tent anyway. Every Thursday night the parish organizes a free potluck dinner for all the hikers in town. It was all over by the time I showed up, but there was a lot of food left and one parishioner showed up late to drop off a homemade cherry pie just as I walked in. He gave me the whole pie, which I ate along with plenty of the leftovers. I was able to get a hot shower, and my stomach was full.

There was a gazebo out back where hikers were allowed to set up their tent. To get to the lawn I had to go down a long stairway. The stairs were very slippery, and I fell for the fifth time that day and went all the way down. I got hurt quite badly. I got a nasty cut on my arm—it was bleeding quite a bit. My ribs hurt a lot, and I broke a strap on my backpack. I managed to get my tent set up, but I was in a lot of pain. Once in my tent I was able to fix my backpack. I limped back into the bunkhouse ate some more food and got my phone and battery charger all charged up while I hung out with other thru hikers. I met another Canadian called Screaming Eagle that night. He had been sick for a few days and had to visit a clinic because he suspected he had Lyme disease. He had found a dead tick on his back earlier that week.

The next morning, I was sore all over from the fall, but I was able to walk. I restocked in a local convenient store, had breakfast, and got on my way. The more my body warmed up, the less the pain got, and I was able to make it through the day. The second morning after my birthday, I was feeling much better and kept on hiking. I found out from Lucille that people back home did not believe I would last this long on the trail. Most of the folks expected me to spend a couple of weeks out here and then return home. My closer friends and family had more faith in me and knew I was resilient.

Chapter 14

Reflecting Back

Being alone on the trail for such a long time gives a person a chance to reflect on all the decisions—good or bad—they made in life. I had been able to reflect on my life during the long training sessions while getting ready for the marathon and Ironman, but it was nothing like spending months alone in the wilderness. Some days I would get a bit depressed because I had let down my wife and kids but then I would always turn to positive thoughts, knowing I had eventually turned my life around. I tried to figure out what caused me to get out of control, but the only thing I could think of is that I have an addictive personality. An addiction is not something that a person plans on, but having a certain personality trait, it just happens. Without the distraction in the everyday world, it is easy to go back in time and let thoughts of the past resurface. Sometimes the memories hurt and sometimes they are pleasant.

Every night on the trail I would think how happy I was that I had finally stopped drinking. I knew that everything

I had done since I stopped would not have been possible if I had kept on abusing alcohol. I just felt sad that I had not quit ten years earlier or better yet that I had never started in the first place. I had never planned to be a drunk. I never planned to hurt my wife and children. It just happened and then it was too late. Maybe if I had known that enjoying a beer would have led to addiction I may have avoided alcohol when I was young, but you never think it can happen to you. I figured it wouldn't happen to me because I was strong and smart. I had three uncles who were alcoholics. I should have seen the signs early on, but I was smart and arrogant. One of my grandfathers also had a hard time controlling his liquor. If he opened a bottle, he had to finish the last drop that night. So I should have known. If I have one drink even now, I know it will lead to many more before it's over, so I have to avoid drinking at all cost.

As a child I could spend hours by myself and always loved spending time in nature. I always dreamed I would be a professional hockey player when I grew up like most kids in Canada did at the time. I would never let anybody bully me around and would fight if I had to. I remember in my first year in school a bully tried to push me around. I got in a fist fight and gave him a black eye. We both got punished by the teacher, but after that day the rest of the class respected me. I also learned quickly to make friends with the older and stronger kids in school. A couple of times, I am ashamed to say, I bullied some weaker kids, but in general, I was always respectful of others.

As a teen I was a decent athlete and did very well in school. I was popular with my friends. I started to drink at school dances when I was just sixteen. The first time I got drunk, other than the sips I took from my dad's bottle, was when we managed to get a bottle from one of my friend's sister. She was old enough to buy booze for us. I felt good for about an hour, but then I got very sick and vomited all over my buddy dad's car. I did not drink again for maybe a year, but the second time I did, I got so drunk I had one of the worst hangovers in my life. I knew right then I had to learn to manage my liquor and I did. I learned how to get just drunk enough to have fun but not go over the limit where I was sick. Unfortunately I was not able to achieve my goal all the time and I did get sick from time to time, but I figured it was part of having fun. Some of my friends were always drunk, so I could justify being hungover once in a while.

My mother was very sad when I came home from university after just one month and told her I was quitting. I was never one to quit easily, but I also know when it's time to move on. I had gone to university to please my mother because she kept saying I was talented in school, and I should not waste my intelligence. At the time, I was not ready for university, but I did not want to disappoint her. So I had applied and had been accepted. I learned a few valid lessons from that experience. Sometimes it's better to quit than to follow someone else's dream. It's also good to make the right decisions for yourself and not let yourself be influenced by others. After I quit, I started collecting unemployment insurance but only had enough for three months. After that I started searching for work. At the time being French Canadian in New Brunswick made it hard to get a job. When I got to my first interview, the manager refused to talk to me when he saw I was French. I eventually got a job and worked in a warehouse for two years before deciding I needed a career. I got accepted at a community college and graduated a couple years later as an electronics technician. I never collected unemployment again.

Every time I met a young thru hiker who had just finished high school, I was amazed. At that age I was not brave enough to attend a university that was only two hours away from my home. My original plan was to go away to study, but I was too chicken to do it. On the trail I would meet many young guys and even gals that had saved up their money and left the comfort of their homes to go on this epic journey. For me doing the trail was an enormous undertaking but to see these young people, even girls still in their teens, have so much courage was inspiring. I would always ask them how their parents felt about their adventure as I would have been concern if one of my children would have done it at that age. I now see how much better they will be in the future if they can adjust back to normal life.

Depression like addiction is also something that a person cannot control. I have always been a very positive person. I always tried to see the positive in any situation. I always tried to use bad experiences as a way to learn. But during the last few years I was drinking I got very depressed. At that time I don't know if I was drinking because I was depressed or if I was depressed because I was drinking. I knew they were related, though, and I had no control over either.

A few years back, I had to take away my dad's driving permit as he progressed with Alzheimer's. He was also not in control. Although he was a very smart and a strong man, the disease had taken over, and there was nothing he could do about it. I had to take him to the hospital one night when he got violent with my mom. He was a very peaceful and kind man. I had never seen him have a fight with my mother while I was growing up. They had to lock him up in a room with no furniture, not even a chair. It was awful, and he did not even know why he was there. He thought he had done something wrong and was being punished in a prison. When I would visit, he would ask me why he could not go back to his apartment. I would try to explain, but his disease had advance so much; he couldn't comprehend.

After he was evaluated and they determined it was no longer safe for him to be left with my mom, I had to take him to a nursing home. He could see that all the other patients at that home were sick and would ask us why he had to stay there. He would tell us that all the folks where he was staying were strange. At first, he thought he was the manager and was controlling the hospices. He was no longer in control. I am glad that I was sober by then so that I could do the little bit I could for him. The night before he died, I sat with him through the night and was hoping and praying it would be his last. When he passed, I was happy because I knew his suffering was finally over.

After watching my father lose control, I can see how hard it must have been for my wife. She had joined Al-Anon, a fellowship group for friends and family of alcoholics, and went through therapy sessions to help her deal with her suffering and to better understand alcoholism. But the real cure for her was to leave me or for me to get sober.

While hiking, I often wondered what my life would have been like if I had not become an alcoholic. I suspect I would have been like most of my friends from high school. I know the strength I got from overcoming my addiction has made me so much stronger, more resilient and determined than I ever was before I became an alcoholic. However, I would much rather never have done the Ironman and marathons and not hurt my family. It's now all in the past, and I have to look at the positive side. The last thing I can do is dwell on the past, and the best thing I can do is look at the future. I told a few people on the trail, people are living longer than ever before, but still every hour that goes by is an hour less to live. I know that may sound morbid, but it can motivate you to take advantage of every moment and live for what lies ahead and let the past be just that. If there is something in life that you want to do, don't let time be the thing that will stop you.

Many people believe that addiction is just a lack of willpower. I can assure you that I have more willpower than most people I have ever met, but I could not control the influence alcohol had over me. I had to fight so hard and long to break the dominance that booze had on me. The love I had for my wife and family eventually helped me defeat the demon, but I had to hit the bottom of the barrel before I could find the first rung on the ladder to climb out. Some addicts do not have to sink so low before they come out and others never do come out of that dark hole. I was one of the lucky ones who had so much support at home to help me fight through it.

On the trail I was a kid again without a care in the world. It was so peaceful and pure. The scenery was beautiful and new over every mountain and with each setting sun. I could hear the birds sing and the sound of the wind. Everything smelled so good. My senses were being reawakened at age sixty-three. I was breathing fresh air and my thoughts were clear. It brought me back to my childhood when we would go play in the woods behind the house, and I never wanted to go back home. Home was a good place with great parents, but in the woods I was free.

Chapter 15

New York

After leaving Pennsylvania it rained for another three days. The rocks did not magically disappear, but they did quickly become more manageable once I was in New Jersey. I was still relishing my time in the wilderness. It was June 1, 2018; I was carrying more food and eating enough to hold my weight constant. I no longer expected trail magic because I had heard that further north there were fewer trail angels. To my surprise, though, I got more trail magic in the north than I did in the south. At noon one day at a road crossing, there was cooked chicken breasts, fresh fruits, and drinks by an angel called Fresh Ground. He claimed he had been called by God to follow hikers on the AT for a year and help them complete their journey by giving them food. It was the best chicken sandwich I had on the trail. I ate so much and was stuffed for the rest of the day. I took my time hiking that day and spent time relaxing by a beautiful pond. I hoped to see him again since he was jumping back and forth at various places to feed hungry hikers, but I never did.

It seemed like every time we crossed that imaginary state line in the woods, the terrain would change along with the state. New York had a lot of very steep but short ups and down. One day I was low on water because I had forgotten to replenish at the last water source. There is a summit in New Jersey where you can see the outline of New York City. There was a girl sitting on a bench having a cold beer, and she had a bottle of water at her side. I sat with her for a while and we talked about whatever. She had a lot of questions about the AT and about thru hiking. She told me that I had inspired her and she now wanted to hike the AT the next year. She said she had wanted to do the Pacific Crest Trail after seeing a movie called *Wild* and also mentioned she was not happy with her life. After a while I asked her if she had water to spare, and she gave me her two-liter bottle since her car was only an hour away and she would be okay without it. When I left, she said I had been sent to her to as an inspiration and that she now had a clear vision for the future. As for me, I got some water I desperately needed that afternoon and had enjoyed spending a couple hours with good company. I am not sure if she ended up hiking the trail, but I was happy to be able to influence her in wanting to do it.

One morning later that week I met Turtle, a hiker going south. He had a busted lip and scratches all over his face and was dirty, as are all the hikers out here. Strange as it may seem, about an hour later he passed me as I was sitting down having a snack. He stopped for a rest and said he had had a bad fall the day before and got hurt quite badly. He was afraid he had broken a tooth, but it turned out that he was just busted up. He said he had gone off the trail to relieve himself that morning and when he got back on the trail he took off in the wrong direction. He walked south for about a half hour before he realized he was heading the wrong way. He was meeting many NOBOs that he had seen before. He asked me which direction was north just to confirm. We became good friends and hiked together for several days. I wanted to hike longer in the day than he did, so we decided to split after a few days. He also was running low on food and had to hitch into town. I offered him some food, but he said he wanted to go for a good meal at a restaurant.

It is amazing how much a person opens up to a complete stranger when hiking together for a few days on the trail. I told him about my problem with alcohol. That was the first time ever I talked about my addiction with a stranger or even to a friend. I felt relieved to be able to share with him something that was deep in me. I also talked about many other personal issues that I had through the years. It was a few days of therapy to be able to openly talk about it without being judged. He helped me a lot without realizing it. He also opened up about many of his personal issues. He said it had been good for him to share his experiences with me also. I probably helped him a lot with his issues. We built an amazing trust between us, and after only a few days.

That same week I met an incredible and inspiring eighteen-year-old young man named Jeremy who was doing the whole portion of the International AT, which starts way down in Florida and goes up to Newfoundland. Just doing the regular AT is challenging enough, but he was doing a whole lot more. When a person hikes the AT, there is a lot of support on the way. There are a lot of hikers and many trail towns. But on the IAT there are a lot fewer hikers to help with issues. You can go for long sections without seeing another soul. The towns north and south of the AT are not as familiar with hikers, so it's a lot harder to hitch a ride. I thought he was extremely courageous to undertake such a journey at such a young age.

Early on in my hike, I was leapfrogging with spring. I tried to do the same with summer, but it seems summer came very fast when I hit New York. It was early June, and we started to see a lot of black flies and many hikers were getting ticks on them. Some folks had to abandon their hike because of scurvy. They were not eating enough fresh fruits. Others got giardia because they were not filtering their water. I also started hearing of people getting norovirus, but it was not spreading too much. I was trying to avoid the shelters even more than before. The only way I would stop at a shelter was if that was the only place to get water. On most of the trails they recommend using the privies, which are at the shelters, to attend to your needs. If you have to go when there are no privies around, then the proper procedure is to dig a cat hole about six inched deep and cover your stool. Because privies are normally filled with germs, I preferred to dig than to use them.

Before Turtle went to town, he told me that the day before we met, they had to chase a mother bear with her cubs away from a shelter after she managed to get into a hiker's food bag one evening. One of the hikers had not properly hung his food bag at that shelter. She had come back several times during the night and even returned in the morning after sunrise. All the hikers were yelling and screaming at the sow to chase her away. He said it was scary and some hikers had a very close encounter when she bluff attacked a couple times. Once a bear eats human food, they are always looking for more.

The morning after I split with Turtle, I did not see anybody till seven in the evening. I met a gentleman in his sixties on top of a mountain having a tuna sandwich. He was playing a guitar and singing at the top of his lungs. After talking for a while, he told me he had started a thru hike in February but had suffered a stroke on the trail and had to be hospitalized. He had a speech impediment and was hard to understand, but he was nice. He said he did not want to sleep around shelters anymore because the night before he was playing his guitar and singing and after about eight songs a hiker threatened to use his guitar as firewood and burn his tent if he played another song. I can understand why they wanted him to stop since he was just learning to play and was not very good. He told me the next day he was getting off the trail to go play at a blues festival. I wished him well and continued to find a good site to set up my tent for the evening.

In the warmer weather it was nice to sleep at night. It was not too hot, and I no longer had to sleep at lower elevations. I would camp along ponds or lakes and enjoyed the sunsets and sunrises because I could just sit without freezing my butt off. And it was warm enough that I could just jump in a lake with my clothes on and bathe and do laundry at the same time, for free. I would try to get a shower whenever I went through parks or tourist areas with facilities. I tried to charge my phone and battery charger at any occasion I got and tried to do my laundry at least weekly. I especially wanted to wash my socks since I only had two pairs and wanted to avoid getting blisters if I could. If socks are not washed regularly with detergent, they get very coarse. One thing I noticed anytime I was able to get a shower, the mosquitoes attacked me a lot more for a few days afterward. It was funny, because like the mosquitoes I could smell a day hiker coming before he got close to me, but I could not smell thru hikers even if they had not had a shower in weeks. I was normally up by five in the morning or even earlier. As soon as the birds started to chirp, I would wake up. It had been over three weeks since I spent a night in a bed, and although I had to fix my mattress almost every other day, I was quite content to sleep in my tent. I was really getting very in tune with nature.

It was easy to know when it was the weekend with the influx of day hikers on the trail. I met a lot of section hikers who were doing a different section every year until they completed the whole trail. Most people on the trail were polite and respectful of other hikers. I also started to hit another bubble of hikers who had started earlier than me and were hiking at about my pace by that point. There were very few NOBO thru hikers left on the trail, but those who were still hiking were all in pretty good trail shape.

Connecticut was a short state and relatively flat, so it went by fast. Besides seeing Screaming Eagles again, I met Hawk, Eagle, Jurassic II, Transformer, Land Fill, Sunshine, and a few others from that new bubble. A new trail family was forming since we were pretty much all at the same pace now. Most of them were much younger than me, ranging from late teens to early forties.

Most backpackers have a trail name, and hikers along the way tried to give me one, but I did not like the names they offered. I just went by Louis, or most friends called me Lou. I finally thought of an appropriate name: Wolf. A wolf in French is a *loup*, and since I was called Lou, I took the name Wolf. Everybody embraced my new name and from then on that's what I was called. It felt strange at first to hear somebody call me Wolf, and it took me a few days to get accustom to my new name.

I met a grumpy old doctor named Doc one evening. He had started in New Jersey and was going north. It was getting quite late that night and since we had to tent in designated areas in Connecticut, I stopped in at a tent site. The site had about five nice spots for tents, but right in the middle was a bear bag hanging only about six feet above ground. There was only one other tent around, and it was in the woods nearby. I went over and asked if it was his bear bag and if he could move because it was in the middle of the campsite. He admitted he should have hung it at a better place but figured since he had gotten to the spot late nobody else would be coming after him. As he started to move his bear bag, he was complaining that a young girl (Sunshine) had gone running by about five minutes before and said she was going to get hurt. He moved his bear bag only about fifteen feet away from my tent and hung it again only about six feet in the air. I tried to offer advice about properly hanging a food bag, but he just wanted to get back to writing his journal and could not be bothered. I bet a bear eventually got his food before he was done with his hike.

All his clothes were hung on a clothesline to air out for the night. I told him it looked like rain was coming, but he ignored me. About twenty minutes later he was scrambling to gather all his clothes when it started to downpour. He was up earlier than me the next morning trying to dry his soaked clothes by a fire. He never even replied the next morning when I greeted him. Some folks are miserable in their own way and it takes more than a few hundred miles of trail to reset their attitude. I never saw Doc again.

I have lots of relatives in Connecticut and had planned to take a side trip to go visit them when I got to that state. The weather was great, warm in the daytime and cooler at night. I was making excellent time and wanted to get home as soon as I could, so by the time I went through Connecticut, I decided to keep on hiking. I was also hoping to be off the trail before the hot and muggy days of summer—and the black flies got really bad—so I wanted to go as fast as possible.

One day I stopped at a grocery store to buy some food. It was the most expensive stop I had seen, but they had the best selection of trail food yet. The folks in the store were very friendly, but the facility was not really hiker friendly. Most of the stores I stopped at had a place where I could charge my equipment while I shopped.

Here they had no outlet to charge my phone and my batteries were getting low. I was having pizza outside when a couple on bicycles stopped to talk with me. I informed them I was looking for an outlet to charge my cell phone. It was a Saturday afternoon and the local library was closed. They were quite nice, and the man said his truck was just around the corner and that I could charge my phone in the truck auxiliary plug. They waited with me for about three hours while I got some charge on my phone. Later that afternoon before leaving town, I saw a cemetery along the trail and found a spare outlet outside, so I sat in the cemetery and finished charging my battery pack and cell phone. I had good reception, so I called home and had a long chat with Lucille without having to worry about using all my power since I was still plugged in. With everything fully charge I was now good for a week without having to worry about finding the next charging station.

When I started the hike, I figured I would have to go home after sixty or seventy days to go pick up my medication and then return to the trail. Instead Lucille was able to ship my meds to me along the way so I could keep on going. When I picked up my meds at the post office in Connecticut, it felt like I had hit a jackpot. My wife had also sent me some homemade protein bars along with a variety of nuts. I had also got a new pair of shoes, so I had everything I needed. At home, I always misplace my glasses, but on the trail, I was still using the first pair that I started with. I had brought a spare pair with me and had arranged to get some shipped, but I was still okay. At the pace I was going I expected to be done in less than a month, by early July, but I knew that the White Mountains in New Hampshire were coming. Everybody talks about the Whites and how difficult they are. I knew it was going to slow me down, but I did not know just how much. I also knew the bug season was upon us and the hot and humid weather was just around the corner. At that time Lucille was trying to predict my finishing date, but I kept advising her that the Whites were coming.

Chapter 16

Massachusetts – Vermont

When I reached Massachusetts it was good because the state has a lot more lakes than the previous states along the AT. With some peaks over three thousand feet, I was getting some nice views again. And by now I was quite comfortable hitchhiking into town, so I could get in quickly, charge my phone as I was doing my laundry or getting a meal, reload on food, and head right back to the trail. At that time I was craving eggs and yogurt, so I would usually buy six eggs, three tubs of yogurt, and some orange juice as soon as I reached a grocery store. I always tried to eat before shopping for groceries to avoid impulse buying and end up with too much food for my pack. I had a list of what I needed and stuck to the list. I was not worrying much about anything anymore. I was now thriving and was experiencing a fantastic adventure.

Not many people bothered me on the trail, and later in the hike I cared even less about what other hikers were doing. I met a man in his fifties who had left Springer the same day I did about three hours before me. I had not seen him before till Massachusetts. I couldn't decide if I liked him or would prefer to avoid him. I had seen him on and off for a couple weeks now and still had a strange feeling about him. He was ranting mostly about his hiking ability.

One morning I had been hiking for about five miles when I ran into him. He was just leaving camp and told me he was only hiking twenty miles per day at present. He said a couple of young hikers who were at the same shelter as him the night before were mouthing off about how good they were. He told me he put them in their place by telling them how much faster he was, and they were only in their twenties. I hiked with him for about an hour. It was all good even though we were having a conversation mostly about him, and I was not that interested with his life to be honest. I told him I needed to take a food break. I figured he would join me to continue our conversation, but he kept on hiking. I caught up to him later as he was filtering water by a brook. "Was I pushing you too hard back there at your age?" he asked. I just smiled and kept on going. Later around noon he leapfrogged me again as I was having my lunch, and he started lecturing me that I was anti-social because I did not eat at the shelters with the rest of the folks on the trail. He told me I was hiking all wrong and that I should learn to backpack properly. I just ignored his comment, figuring he obviously had an issue he had not worked out yet. Now I knew I did not like him.

I probably passed him while he had stopped at the shelter because around three that afternoon he passed me again as I was filtering water at a spring just before a big climb. While hiking up the mountain, I noticed he was struggling, and I walked right pass him and smiled as I went by. I normally don't act that way, but he had gotten under my skin that day. He tried to keep up with me, but I left him far behind. It felt kind of good to show off, but I felt a little bad at the same time. I stopped at the trailhead at the top to sign in at the trail registry. He went by without saying a word. After I caught up to him again at the next climb, he said, "you probably want to go by," knowing he had been mocked. I informed him I was good and would hike with him. I figured we would have a normal conversation.

I was wrong. He started to tell me I had to do the Pacific Coast Trail (PCT) the following year because he was going to do it. He also told me he was going to be a Triple Crown Hiker, even though he had not finished his first long-distance hike. A Triple Crown is completing all three long-distance hikes in the US: the PCT, the AT, and the Continental Divide Trail. He was trying his best to get back at me by trying to bully me, but he stopped at a shelter for the night and I kept on going. To my surprise before we parted ways, he told me that he was inspired that I had such endurance at my age—however, he did reemphasized that I was hiking wrong and should change my ways. I just laughed to myself and continued for another four miles that night.

On the afternoon of Sunday, June 11, 2018, I walked through a busy park in Massachusetts and figured I would stop at a porta potty. After going about my business in nature for a few months, I figured it would be nice to use a toilet. I almost lost my diner because it was so gross. It made the privies on the trail look like five-star toilets. I can't imagine how a nice public park could have such filthy potties. It was the busiest section of the trail with many local walkers. All the folks in the park were quite friendly. One woman, after seeing my backpack, asked me if I was looking for trail magic. Every thru hiker will answer that question with an enthusiastic "YES." She gave me everything she had in her day pack including two fresh avocados. I had never eaten fresh avocado before, and they were so good that afternoon. I started buying a couple avocados after that whenever I saw them.

Trail magic was happening more and more often as we were hiking north. One man stopped at a road crossing one afternoon and asked what we were doing. He was the CEO of a big construction company and said he had always wanted to find out what all these people with big backpack were doing. I explained about the AT, thru hikers, and about trail magic. He told me to stay there; he would be back in five minutes. When he got back, he filled my backpack with bars, chip, and fruits. He said he would start to do trail magic on a weekly basis to help hikers. He had hiked on the trail before and was aware of its existence but had never talked to a thru hiker before and had not heard the AT went from Georgia to Maine and that folks would actually go all the way. We talked for over an hour but then I told him I had to keep on moving. He was impressed with my story and after our discussion he was interested to find out a more about the trail and ATC, and he said he would consider hiking it when he retired.

Another evening I met a local couple with a small day pack. I would always try to engage people in a conversation if they had a small pack because I figured they might have some fresh fruits. This couple did not have any fruit, but the woman said she knew how much hikers appreciated food along the trail. She said her son had done part of the AT the year before but quit after he became homesick. She said she always had a couple fresh batches of homemade cookies and offered a bag of either chocolate chip or molasses cookies. I was torn with the decision since I liked both of them, so I asked if I could get one of each. I felt greedy, but I left with a big smile on my face. It was always fun to get extra food because I was always hungry no matter how much I ate. That's what they call hiker hunger.

Many thru hikers I talked to said how much the hike had restored their faith in humanity. They could not understand why some complete strangers would go out of their way to help. It wasn't a big surprise to me because I had been a volunteer firefighter for over thirty-five years. Regularly I saw people get up in the middle of the night to respond to an alarm and go help a complete stranger in distress. Still I felt humbled by the kindness of the people in the trail towns along the AT. Quite often we would get to a road crossing and find a cooler full of sodas or beers and fresh fruits and also a place to dump our trash.

I met with Screaming Eagle just outside Williamstown, Massachusetts, late in the afternoon on June 13, and we decided to spend the night at the first campsite in Vermont. There are different rules for camping in Vermont. It seems that every state had different rules for back country camping. I think they do that just to confuse thru hikers. Kidding, aside we knew there was a big campsite coming up soon. With very few thru hikers left on the trail going our speed, we figured there would be no problem getting a good tent spot. To our surprise, when we got to the campsite there were over twenty tents already in the campsite. A strange fellow came to talk to me, so I asked him what was going on. He said "did you not get the memo? This is the hiking season. I have been here for three nights, and it's been like this every night. I have been on the trail for six days already"

He tried to help me find a good flat spot and wanted to help me put my tent up. I think he was bored while waiting for an injury to recover. I told him I was okay to set up my tent alone and that I had been on the trail for over three months. As it so happened, it was peak season for Long Trail thru hikers. The Long Trail starts near the border of Massachusetts and goes for about 273 miles to the Canadian border. It coincides with the AT in Vermont for about hundred miles. So for the next hundred miles all the campsites would be crowded, and the trail would be busy. Hikers do the LT in both directions in late spring.

I was glad after we were done the section that coincided with the LT because there were fewer hikers on the trail, which made it easier to find a good flat site to pitch our tents at night. The weather had been warmer and water sources were not as reliable as before. I had to carry more water to make sure I would not run out. The only concern I had was that I knew the Whites were coming soon, and I knew they were going to be tough.

On a beautiful afternoon after crossing into Vermont, I stopped for a rest and late snack next to a beautiful pond. There was a shelter about three hundred yards off trail, and since it was a warm sunny afternoon, a lot of hikers were enjoying the water. I talked to a young Canadian girl that had hiked most of the trail the year before. She had skipped Vermont and jumped to Maine to get to Katahdin because her visa was about to expire. About thirty-five miles from Katahdin, she fell and broke her wrist and needed an operation, so she could not finish the hundred mile wilderness and reach the summit. She was back to finish two sections that she could not complete in 2017 and achieve her dream of completing the AT.

Late that evening I reached the park where I had planned to spend the night before a big climb in the morning. There were signs all over saying overnight camping was not allowed in the park. I was not sure what I was going to do when I heard a familiar voice coming through the woods. It was Eagle, an eighteen year old guy that I met earlier and hadn't seen for about a week. It was like that on the trail; I met friends, and then I would not see them again for days or weeks. He said there was a nice spot next to him where he was stealth camped and we could plead ignorance if we got caught. It was dark already, so I figured it was safe as long as I left early in the morning. He was a pleasant, free spirit and we became good friends. I left early the next morning, and we met on the summit of a ski resort for lunch.

We knew there was a nice lake coming the next day and had talked about going for a swim. When we got to the lake there was a bunch of weekend hikers enjoying the water. It was a very weird group; they had met online and were doing a weekend camping trip. We had a good swim and figured we could score some food from them since they were only there for an overnight trip. I was getting low on food and was not sure I could make it to the next town. I was always taking just enough food to make it to the next town where I would resupply. Eagle was dropping hints, but we were not getting anywhere. Because I was getting cold, I decided to move on. An hour or so later, Eagle caught up with me and told me that they finally understood we were looking for food. He had some energy bars for me. They had invited him to stay for diner and spend the night with them, but he declined.

Later that day when we got to the area where we had planned to spend the night, there was another group already there. It was a group of women, and we could tell by their gestures that we were not welcome to camp around them. They politely told us we needed to find another campsite. I don't know why they felt threatened. Maybe they thought we were up to no good. We did not argue and moved on across the river where another hiker did not want us around either. That was a strange day. It was the first time on the trail that my presence at a camping site was not wanted. We did manage to find a nice tent site and settle for the night. I left early the next morning and did not see Eagle for a few days after that.

Things were going great; I was enjoying the nice weather and was blessed with lots of trail magic. Getting a hitch into towns was a lot easier in the north. Things were going good, too good. I was feeling very good about finishing the trail without any major problems, but while

I was eating a candy, it got stuck in my teeth and cracked one of the teeth holding my bridge my dentist had been concerned about. The fixture was holding for the time being, but it hurt really bad. It was the first major mishap, and I hoped I would not have to go home or to a local dentist to get my teeth repaired.

Chapter 17

New Hampshire

The trail goes through the town of Norwich, Vermont and on June 20, I was on the Vermont-New Hampshire border, and the town made me feel welcomed. Three out of the five first houses I passed offered trail magic. There were coolers with sodas, watermelons, ice water, and homemade bread. Another place had a box loaded with band aids, blister plasters, tampons, and other drug store items. As a hiker, I felt very welcomed in that town. Later that morning a man stopped and offered to buy me coffee and doughnuts at a shop he was going in. I thanked him but told him I was looking for a real breakfast. He told me where I could get a good one in town.

Crossing the border on the bridge into Hanover, New Hampshire, was just as welcoming. I was approached by quite a few people on the street asking me if there was anything I needed and offering to help with a ride and offering me a place to stay for the night.

I had to go to the post office to get a package containing a new pair of shoes and my medication that Lucille had sent. I felt that I now had everything I needed to finish my journey to Maine. There was a great pizza place that offered free pizza to thru hikers. I was looking for eggs but settled for free delicious pizza instead. In Hanover there is a community center where I had a shower and laundry for five dollars, and I could leave my pack there while I did my grocery shopping at a store across the street. I also ate a lot of food at the store, including my regular six boiled eggs. While I was doing laundry, I managed to treat my clothes for the final time with Permethrin that I was able to find locally. I also charged my battery pack, phone, and head lamp while I rested for most of the afternoon. It was a nice day, perfect for standing out in the sun to dry my clothes after spraying them.

As I relaxed on a park bench waiting for my clothes to dry out, a retired gentleman approached me and offered me some energy bars. He mentioned he often helps out hikers with food or lodging. When he found out I was from Canada and that I played hockey as a youth, he wanted to help me even more. He informed me he had coached hockey at a high level; it was his passion. We talked for a couple hours about all the players that had come from the region and became pro or played high-level hockey. He was quite passionate about local players too. He really loved the game. After a while he went back to his home and returned with a lot more energy bars. He loaded me up with bars and cookies. He was a card collector and he showed me some signed player's cards he was quite proud of. It had been a pleasant afternoon talking hockey. Norwich and Hanover were by far the most hiker-friendly towns I had been through. I never felt so welcomed in any other places on the AT.

One morning, as I walked across a road, somebody yelled at me. It was Carl Spring, a trail angel, with a pickup truck. He had a propane burner in the back and offered to make me an omelet with cheese and peppers. He had just finished cooking breakfast for Jurassic II, another hiker that was attempting to complete his last section of the AT. He was from Switzerland and had started his hike in 2008 and was doing a section almost every year since he had started.

Carl cooked me an omelet made with six eggs along with six pieces of toast, four bananas, and lots of orange juice. He said he was retired and every day from late May to late September he was setting up with food to help hikers. He wanted to hike the trail, but he was too afraid of snakes. Instead he helped hikers with food or other needs and expected nothing in return, but he enjoyed hearing our stories. For him it was rewarding to help us accomplish our goal, and for hikers like me it was awesome. He also had a couple of really nice dogs with him. I talked for over two hours about my adventure. His wife showed up after a while, and we all sat and talked.

Now I was about to hit the Whites Mountains with their beautiful scenery and challenging climbs. As the climbs were getting harder, the rewarding views at the summits were getting even better. Climbing Mt. Moosilauke was the hardest climb I had done so far on the AT. I hiked from approximately one thousand feet to almost five thousand feet at the summit. It was a very steep climb compared to previous mountains. I was finally into bigger mountains and tougher terrain. My only problem at the time was my loose denture. The pain had resided, and I hoped it would hold till the end of the journey.

My expectation of the White Mountains did not deceive me. I expected them to be tough, and very early into New Hampshire I knew I was in for some very hard hiking miles ahead. I went from averaging twenty-five miles per day to struggling to achieve on average of about eighteen. I was hiking a lot harder and taking shorter breaks during the day, but my mileage was still dropping. I also had to be a lot more aware of where I was selecting a campsite in the evening because in the Whites it was much harder to find a good flat spot on the side on the ridges to pitch a tent. In the south they call the low elevation between mountains a *gap* while in the north it's called a *notch*. I asked local hikers why it had a different name. Everybody had a different opinion, but nobody knew for sure. They all said, "that's what we've always called them."

In the White Mountains there is a range of mountains called the Presidential Range. They are amongst the highest peaks in New Hampshire, and most summits are named after American presidents. One morning when I was climbing the Presidential Range, I reached into my pocket and realized I had lost my knife. I needed it to cut tape to fix the leaks in my defective sleeping pad. I stopped on top of a mountain to enjoy the view, and there were a few women enjoying their lunch. It was a clear day, and we could see all the Presidential peaks, including Mount Washington. I had asked the ladies if I could join them while I dried my tent and ate my lunch. I had a bottle of fresh maple syrup that I had bought at the previous town. The bottle was supposed to last me four or five meals, but it was so good it was all gone by the end of that lunch.

The women were all very interested in my story like most day hikers normally are. When they asked if I was doing okay, I told them I was having a great time and felt good but that I lost my knife that morning. Without losing a beat one of the ladies told me she had two knives and only needed one. I figured she did not have two since she was just on a day hike and just made that up in order to make it easy for me to take her knife. I was grateful since

I really needed a knife. It was trail magic at its best. As they say, "The trail provides."

I did not tell them I was starting to struggle because my right knee was swelling up and hurting. Going up and down the big boulders in the White Mountains was starting to take its toll on me physically and mentally. I was starting to struggle with my hike.

I had not spent a night in a shelter since Harpers Ferry. It was getting late and I knew I could not make it down the mountain before dark. Also the descent coming up was one of the most challenging ones on the whole AT. It was dangerous even in the daylight. I had to set up camp next to a shelter. It was the weekend so there were many weekend and overnight hikers. I had to set up in an uneven spot with lots of rocks. I knew I was going in town the next morning because I was about to run out of food. I had not seen Jurassic in a while, so I set up my tent next to his so we could have a chat. He informed me that a local hiker called Chris had offered him a ride into town and suggested I might be able to get a ride with them.

The next morning when I got up Jurassic was already up and ready to leave. He told me Chris had left very early and was waiting for him at the trailhead parking lot to give him a bottle of fuel. He told me he was good on food and had decided he was not going into town because all he needed was fuel. I was not yet ready to leave so I told him not to worry about me; I would hitch a ride. When I got to the trailhead, I was surprised to see Chris and Jurassic. They were waiting for me and Chris offered to drive me into town. He dropped me off at a grocery store right next to the laundry. When I asked him how hard it was to get a ride back to the trailhead, he gave me his phone number and told me to call him when I was done with my laundry and shopping and that he would gladly drive me back to the trailhead.

I bought my usual six boiled eggs, yogurt and orange juice plus a few chicken breasts and gathered some change to do the laundry next door. Before I could start my laundry, Chris showed up and told me we could go to his house since he was just chilling that morning. He said I could do my laundry and shower there. I had a great morning. It was the first time I had been in a real house since Virginia. I showed him how to tie flies for fly fishing, and we told each other fishing stories all morning. It was great to sit on a sofa and relax all morning. It is amazing the things we take for granted in normal civilization. It was also good to be able to rest my knee. After resting all morning Chris dropped me back at the grocery store where I stocked up on food and had lunch while he went to pick up another hiker at another trailhead.

After he came back and picked me up, he offered to take me to a restaurant. I knew I could eat again and was thinking I could buy him lunch to repay all his kindness. At the restaurant he said he wanted to pay, and yet I was the one that wanted to treat him. He said it would not be right to do trail magic and expect a meal in return, so I let him pay. I was being pushed totally out of my comfort zone. After he drove me back to the trail head, I took some pictures, and we exchange phone numbers. He said if I needed anything till I reached Maine, that he was just a phone call away. It had been another one of those memorable days along the journey. Chris helped me a lot and showed me how much I missed the luxury of home. It was hard to be back on the trail hiking that afternoon after spending most of the day in a home.

Hawk, a hiker I met, who had completed a thru hike a few years before, was always talking about Franconia Ridge and how nice it was. He said no matter how long it would take or what he had to do, he would wait for a sunny day to go over the ridge. When I got to that climb, it was a cloudy and rainy day. I decided I was not waiting for the weather to clear against Hawk's advice. It was the first section where I was going to be above the tree line for a long distance. Since there was no thunder, I felt safe to continue. When I got up on the ridge, I got lucky when the clouds cleared for about twenty minutes. I did not get to walk the whole ridge under a clear sky, but I was fortunate enough get a glance at what Hawk described. It was spectacular.

In the Presidential Range, there is a system of huts that are managed by the Appalachian Mountain Club to cater to tourist hikers. The huts are more like lodges and are located within distances that can easily be hiked in a day. You can make reservations for a place to stay that includes a fine dining and a good breakfast. It is quite popular amongst tourists, and it is a good way to introduce hiking, and to some degree backpacking, to people. In the evening guides give lectures on various topics. The huts are based after the European models. They are too expensive for most thru hikers on a budget, though, and I was no exception.

Hikers are not allowed to tent within a quarter mile of the huts. Also in New Hampshire it is illegal to set up your tent above the tree line. If you happen to get to a hut after four in the afternoon, the first hiker to arrive can stay in exchange for cleaning the rooms in the morning, help with dishes, and other chores around the huts. There is usually one spot for a thru hiker per night. I was not interested in that option because you can only leave late in the morning after all the guests have eaten and checked out for the day. However, if a thru hiker shows up to the hut after the patrons are done eating, they will offer you all the leftovers for free. I always found the workers quite friendly and took advantage of the leftovers. They also have clean washrooms and potable water at all the huts so that hikers can fill their bottles.

Before I started through the Presidential Range, I was not aware that food would be available at the huts and that you could buy energy bars at them. It was the toughest section of the trail so far. I knew I was going to be hiking much slower than usual, so I took more food than I needed for that section just to be safe. That was a mistake because my pack was heavier than ever.

I had met an eighteen year old girl a while back in Pennsylvania. She was very strong physically and I thought mentally. She hiked with Hawk most of the time, and at one point they did over thirty miles for eight consecutive days. They were having a break one morning by the side of the trail, and I stopped to talk to them. The girl was crying and told me it was her last day on the trail. She could not take the hike anymore. She had been able to hike only under ten miles per day. I tried to reassure her that it was okay, but Hawk said she had been thinking about stopping as far back as Vermont.

I got to the next hut around noon, right before they did, and was offered the rest of the food. I took some food but told one of the employees that I wanted to leave some for a hiker coming behind me who was having a rough day. When Hawk and the girl arrived, she said she did not want any food. I tried to talk to convince her to take a few days off in a hotel and think about her decision, but she burst into tears again and said her mind was made up; she was going home. I was about to buy a couple of energy bars at the hut before leaving. When she found out I was looking for food she emptied her food bag and told me to take it all. I felt way too guilty, but she insisted. She said I would be doing her a favor because she would rather give it to a friend than dump it in the hiker box. I reluctantly agreed. Once again, my backpack was way too heavy, but if I made her feel better, I was okay with it. Besides I knew it would get light very fast. That was probably my saddest day on the whole journey. It was sad to see such a strong girl abandon her dream, but somehow I knew she was doing the right thing for herself at that moment. It also planted a seed in my mind that quitting was an option that I had not even thought about before.

Chapter 18
The Whites

The Whites were even tougher than I had imagined. I expected the mountains to be hard, but I figured that I would have my trail legs by this point and would easily manage. My thigh muscles were getting really tight, and my right knee was getting quite sore and aching most of the time. Both hips were also locking up and giving me sharp pain at times. I would have to stop and twist and stretch before I could keep on hiking. I carried anti-inflammatory medication in case my arthritis flared up and started taking them for the first time. For the first time since I had left Springer, I was starting to have doubts about being able to complete my epic adventure. Seeing the girl quit messed with my head, and I thought I may also not finish. I was finally starting to break down physically and mentally.

After breakfast one morning I started to look for my toothpaste but could not locate it. Also I noticed that there was a protein bar missing from by food bag. I looked around to see if a raccoon or some other rodent had penetrated my tent, but there were no holes anywhere in the fabric. I did not think more about it till I took my break and went to put my energy bar rappers in my garbage bag. In the bag, I found a partial piece from the missing protein bar along with the wrapper. I also found my empty tube of toothpaste with teeth marks on the container. When I set up my tent that night, I rechecked for holes but everything was intact. Then it dawned on me that if a raccoon had gotten into my food and toothpaste, it wouldn't have put the litter in my garbage. I figured I got hungry during the night and dreamt that the toothpaste was a gel and ate it.

There was an Appalachian Mountain Club (AMC) lodge with a bunkhouse and cabins at a road crossing. Inside the guesthouse there was also a restaurant and a store on the first level, and the basement was open twenty-four hours. In there we could pay for a shower, charge our phones, and dry our clothes. I got there just before the restaurant closed. I had plenty of food. I got a much needed shower (It had been about ten days since I had my last shower). One of the AMC caretakers was chilling out before returning to the shelter he managed. He had access to the company's washing machines and offered to do my laundry. I gratefully accepted. It was good to have clean socks.

In the White Mountains you were restricted from setting up your tent just anywhere. You had to be a mile from a road crossing, a quarter mile from a pond, and at least two hundred feet from the trail. After hiking about a hundred yards from the AMC headquarters, I bumped into Eagle. He had set up his tent right next to the trail across a pond. He claimed he was not aware of the regulations. He was also not aware he could charge his phone back at the AMC center. He left his tent there and returned to the guesthouse to charge his phone. He said people were looking at him strangely as they were passing by his tent, but nobody said anything. It must be nice to be young and worry-free. I went on for another half mile and found a good stealth spot away from the trail and set up for the night.

The reception in the mountains was not very good, so one morning while I stopped to check if there were any leftovers one of the caretakers ask me to transport a note to a girl at another hut up the trail. I was happy to help him out and was very surprised when he gave me a huge piece of ginger cake. I did not expect anything in return but was very pleased. It was the best piece of ginger cake I ever had in my life. It seems everything tastes better when you're hungry. By then I could easily eat seven thousand calories per day and still be hungry.

The Presidential Range is quite beautiful but also very rocky and I did not particularly like them. I have a feeling going through the Presidential for a weekend or section hike would be fun, but for me as a thru hiker, it was just a bit too much. Also there are way too many tourists to have a peaceful day. And a lot of time was spent above the tree line which meant I always had to make sure there were no storms in the forecast. Fortunately the weather was great, and the scenery was remarkable. I also had to make sure I would not get caught above the tree line late in the day. I got to the hut just before Lakes of the Clouds hut just before summiting Mount Washington around three thirty in the afternoon and knew that it was over eight miles to the next camping site below Mount Madison. What I did not know was the kind of terrain that was coming ahead, so I asked one of the caretakers if I could make it before dark. He said it would take me around four hours to get there. It was a very rocky path that never went below the tree line.

Going from Lakes of the Clouds hut to Mount Madison hut was quite an adventure. I met a fellow Canadian from my home province who was doing a southbound thru hike. He was the first hiker from New Brunswick I met on the trail. He was in great spirits and was making good time on his hike. It was nice to speak to another hiker from home. We were starting to meet a lot of SOBO's that had started in Main around the same time as him. Later in the evening, about two hours before I got to the next campsite, I met a couple of hikers in their fifties who were going to the Lakes of the Clouds hut. We were about half way in between the two huts, and they said they wished me luck getting there before nightfall since they had been walking for about five hours. I could tell they were exhausted, so I figured I would not break their hearts by telling them they were only halfway. There was nothing much I could do to help them, so I figured I would not discourage them and tell them what they were in for the rest of the way. I also knew they weren't in danger as they could stop at Mount Washington and take cover for the night. I always wondered if they made it to the hut or had to quit when they got to Mount Washington.

Around sunset I met five young inexperienced hikers climbing the last peak I had just gone over. Since it was starting to get dark, I tried to convince them to turn around and get back to a safe place before nightfall. They insisted on summiting two more mountains before the night. I had just been where they were going, and the wind was picking up and it was getting cold. They were not properly dressed, but no matter how hard I tried to change their mind, they were too stubborn to listen. I am sure they had a very miserable night. I was exhausted by the time I finally got to my camping spot and knew I had pushed myself too much that day. My right knee was hurting and was badly swollen. It had seized up going down to the campsite. I was limping and wasn't sure if I would make it. I figured I would have to take the next day off because I could hardly walk. It had been a very eventful day, and I was seriously thinking I may have to stop and go home. I took some anti-inflammatory pills. I tried to go to sleep, but my tent was not set on a flat spot, so I kept sliding against the side of the tent all night. The next morning my knee was still seriously swollen. The pain was manageable, and I could hike without too much difficulties, though.

Toward the end of the Whites my knee was hurting every night. The end was so close, and yet it was still so far away. I would soak my knee in cold streams everyday as much as I could to keep the swelling down. In the morning it was stiff, but the pain would subside when it warmed up. Then in the afternoon it would hurt again. The black flies were also getting quite bad, and the loneliness was finally getting to me. It was now both a mental and physical struggle to keep on hiking. I still had no plans of quitting, but I was in a bad place. I needed to take a few days off, but I was afraid if I did my muscles would seize up, and I'd be out of commission for a couple of weeks.

I called home and asked Lucille if she wanted to come down for a weekend. There was a holiday coming up, and it was going to be a long weekend in Canada. We could spend the weekend together, and I would get a much needed rest. After some discussion, though, she mentioned that it would be a twelve-hour drive one way, and she would be too tired to make it worthwhile since she would only have one day with me. Besides I was probably just under two weeks to the end, so she told me to take a few days off in a hotel and then keep on hiking after the break. I was disappointed but I totally understood her point. I decided to keep on hiking despite the pain. My morale was as low as it had been since the start. I was enjoying my hike less and less. For the first time, it was more about the destination than the journey.

I got a text from Chris the next day. He wanted to join me for a couple days the coming weekend. It was just what I needed to lift my spirits. I told him where I would be on Friday and that I needed to go into town for supplies. I had very bad cell reception, so I did not hear back from him. I figured if I was hurting too much, I could spend a couple days with him at his home. That Friday morning when I neared the trailhead, I saw somebody coming towards me yelling at me. I did not recognize him or what he was saying till he got close. It turned out he was greeting me. It was Jurassic. Chris took us both into town to get some food and supplies and then drove us back to the trail. After getting back to the trailhead, we dried our gear since it was a sunny morning and had been raining for three days. Eagle also showed up. I thought he was way ahead of me, but he had also gone into town. He was very excited because he had been interviewed by a reporter for a hiking magazine that morning. Chris was having fun catching snakes while we dried our tents. He caught a few and played with them before releasing them back unharmed.

I charged my phone in the car auxiliary adapter. I knew I was going to be at least five days before the next town, so I bought a lot of food and my backpack was quite heavy. Since Chris was only with us for a couple of nights, he offered to carry some of my food for the first day. Jurassic, Chris, and I hiked all day and set up camp along a scenic lake with a splendid view. Eagle was a faster hiker and left before we did, so we never caught up with him. Chris got some bad news that day and had to get back home, so he left early the next morning. He took a side trail to the road and hitched a ride back to his car.

In the Whites we were still meeting SOBO's that had started at Katahdin, Maine. Some were doing great while others were in very bad shape. Almost one in two were wearing a head net to keep the mosquitoes and black flies away. I had not seen a NOBO with a head net yet, so I figured the worst of the blackflies was yet to come. When we asked them if they were going all the way, they replied, "That's the plan." It reminded me how I answered before reaching Harpers Ferry. It was funny, Eagle complained about the SOBO's having way too much energy in the shelters; they had not hiked long enough and were not tired like we were. He joked that the trail angels should put a sign on the trail magic saying "for NOBO's only" because they did not deserve trail magic yet.

With less than two weeks and about two hundred miles to go, I called home when I got to the top of Wildcat Mountain and asked Lucille if she could come and get me in Gorham, New Hampshire, the next day. I had finally broken down mentally and physically. The pain in my knee had gotten so bad and I was concern I that was going to do permanent damage. My mind was being challenged even more than my knee. I figured if I could go home for a couple weeks and rest, maybe I could come back and finish the trail. Home was only about eight hours away, and the thought of resting was taking over my desire to complete without stopping. I told her that my only condition was that I could return and finish the trail at a later date. So Lucille agreed to drive up and pick me up and would allow me to come back and finish the trail in a couple weeks when I was feeling better. I was kind of hoping she would try to talk me out of it and encourage me to keep on going. During my struggles with addiction she was always there for me, and this time was no different. She supported my decision to take a break. I was blessed to have such a wonderful wife I could count on. I felt so fortunate to have married her.

Chapter 19

Maine

That evening while I was having a phone conversation with Lucille, Eagle hiked by, and I only had a quick chat with him since I was on the phone. I had not seen him in about a week, so I told him I would see him at the next spot where he would be tenting. It was already late in the day so I knew he would not get far. The climb down the mountain was more challenging than we had anticipated, so we both had to find a less than desirable place to set up camp for the night. I informed Eagle of about my plan to get off the trail the next day, and that I was mentally exhausted. He totally understood and was very supportive of my decision, knowing I could easily come back when I was feeling better. We talked quite late, and he never even once tried to convince me to keep going. However, just talking to a friend was all I needed to elevate my moral. I was no longer sure if I wanted to quit by the time I went to bed, since I was so close to my destination. The next morning I told Eagle I was continuing the hike. I called

Lucille when I got to the next summit and informed her I was going to make it, and she did not have to come and pick me up. I was still not sure I could make it to the end, but I figured I would take it one day at a time and evaluate my status every night.

Walking into the final state was surreal. I had finally reached the last milestone on the trek, and even though I was injured, I now had a good feeling I would complete my expedition. I was back in a good mental state. The daunting Whites were behind me. I expected this last state to be much easier. I could not have been more wrong. The SOBOs I passed were all scratched up and most were complaining about how hard their hike through Maine had been. They were looking forward to the Whites as much as I was looking forward to conquering Maine. I warned them about the tough terrain ahead, but having completed their first state, they were full of energy. Going southbound is a lot harder because the worst terrain is at the start of the hike.

On June 28, a heat wave hit Maine, and it was nasty. I had walked through a few hot days before, but this was a scorcher. The weather forecast was calling for extreme heat for the coming week. They were advising people to stay inside and avoid exercise. How was I to avoid exercising when I am walking up and down the mountains? The water sources were also getting scarce and most of the smaller streams and springs had dried up.

The hike was still far from over, but at least the fords were going to be easy. There were very few NOBOs left at that point and the few I was seeing were all much younger than I was. I still saw Jurassic and Eagle occasionally and met a few others that I had not met before, Transformer and Landfill. I saw Hawk for the first time in quite a while, and he informed me that he was heading to town like most hikers to get out of the heat.

I made sure I stayed well hydrated, and I even had a small bottle of sea salt to make sure I got enough electrolytes to properly absorb the water. Maine was proving to be a lot more challenging than I had anticipated, with the heat, the nasty roots, and the scrambling rock climbs. I was falling often and was banged and bruised, but I was having fun again. My knee was still hurting quite badly, but it was not getting any worse. I had under two weeks left before I would complete my adventure. The climbs up the mountains may not have been as high as New Hampshire, but they were more technical. And with the heat came extreme thundershowers, which made the rocks very slippery, deer flies and mosquitoes. It was a real challenge, but I had come out of my rut and was in great spirits again.

Maine has a lot of lakes or ponds, as they call them over there. The climbs were tough but the scenery on the summits was for me the best I had seen thus far. With the heat came sunny, clear skies. When I hit a summit, I could enjoy the views even more and could stay on top without freezing my butt off. Since the higher elevation is always cooler, I would try to camp as high as I could below the tree line, which was the opposite of when I started out and camped in the lowest elevations.

Mahoosuc Notch, known as the toughest mile on the AT, was yet to come. It's a deep notch in the Mahoosuc Range in western Maine. You have to climb over boulders bigger than cars with ten feet drops. Everybody I talked to was looking forward to it, but they said not to go through on a rainy day or late in the afternoon. I hit the Notch around four in the afternoon on June 30. I knew I had enough time before sunset to make it through, but I was tired, having hiked almost twelve hours already. It was nothing like I had expected. Up to that point, I had faced extreme climbs or descents that had big drops. I had climbed over boulders before, but this section was different. This felt more like rock climbing. It was more difficult than I had expected. I had to scramble over boulder after boulder. It required much more of my strength to get through. At one point I even had to remove my pack to squeeze through a hole in a crevasse. It was by far the hardest mile I had faced. I would sometimes have to throw my hiking poles down or over the boulders so that I would have both hands free to climb over the rocks.

I went through the Notch with Transformer and Jurassic and one of the strange things in the Notch that amazed us was the temperature drop in the gap. It was at least twenty degrees colder than just a hundred yards before. The drastic drop in temperature was welcoming on that scorcher of a day. There was still snow and ice in the cavities below. It was challenging, but I was having so much fun until I slipped on a rock. I fell in a bad way and broke a couple ribs on my right side. I have broken my ribs numerous times playing hockey or falling while riding mountain bikes. I knew this time they were broken again because I could feel the crepitus when I pushed on them. It is an eerie feeling of bones rubbing against other bones where they are separated. I caught my breath, waited for about five minutes, and then continued on through. Staying there was not an option, so I just had to move on. I was hurting bad, but the pain was not enough to make me want to quit.

My two partners had gone ahead since they were a bit faster than me and were not aware I was hurt. When I finally got through, they were already setting up camp for the night at a nice campsite. There were a few other hikers that had stopped there also. There was a sweet waterfall and it would have been a great spot to spend the night and take a bath, but I decided to keep on moving. I knew there was a thunderstorm coming rather quickly, and I wanted to climb Mahoosuc Arm before the rocks got wet.

Mahoosuc Arm is one of the nastiest summits on the AT, and I figured if I can get as high as possible before the rain, I would be much better off in the morning. My ribs were hurting. While I was warmed up it was manageable, and I did not know how much they would hurt the next morning. I made it over three quarters of the way up before the rain and lightning started. I found a spot with very soft and deep moss. I did not even need a mattress that night. I figured I could sleep well even if I slept on my left side.

It rained very hard that night and the thunder kept waking me up. The next morning I was in bad shape. I now had a knee problem and broken ribs. I could still feel the crackling between the bones but to my surprise the pain was not bad unless I moved in a certain way. I was okay to keep on hiking. I was no longer paying attention to the little problems as I did early on because I now had big problems. So on day one hundred I got my first blister. When I took my shoes off to look, I actually had three places where the skin was peeling on my toes of my left foot and one more on my right foot. They had just appeared out of nowhere, probably because the trail was very muddy that morning, and I had not paid attention to the warning signs. I tried taping them, but that caused friction on my other toes. I was afraid I'd have more chafing. I did not want the open blisters to become infected, so I covered the exposed flesh with some superglue that I had. It worked wonders, and the blisters never bothered me again after that. I should have cleaned my toes before applying the glue. I was worried it would get infected, but at least the blisters were under control.

Despite the heat, my hurting knee, a couple broken ribs, four blisters, and too many bruises to count, I was enjoying myself and cherishing the thought that my adventure was soon coming to an end. I was in a great place and felt at peace. It suddenly felt like each day was going by too fast. I was trying to slow down. Thinking back, the trip felt like a dream. I thought about my childhood and early adult life more than I had done on the whole hike. I was on the last week, and it seemed like everything was coming together and apart at the same time. I was happy and sad at the same time, and I knew if I had not stopped drinking eighteen years before, I would not have been there.

Throughout the AT there are bridges at most river crossing, but in Maine I had to fords many rivers. I would usually remove my socks and put my shoes back on to go across because the rocks were very slippery. I did not have any water shoes. When I got to the other side, I would put my socks back on and hope my shoes would dry eventually. Lucille was aware that the reception would be scarce in Maine, so I hoped she would not be too worried. Most of my gear was coming apart or was broken, and I hoped my fifth pair of shoes would hold till the end.

Chapter 20

The Last Week

I was in a great place mentally as I was expecting to be complete the trail within ten days. The biggest problem at the end was the heat and that it was out of my control. I was about to finish what I had started over a hundred days ago. My water filter system had a hole in the bottle and the filter was clogged up. When it was new it would take me thirty seconds to filter a bottle, by the end it took me a good five minutes, and I had to squeeze really hard. My air mattress would hold air for only about an hour, just long enough for me to get to sleep. My tent was leaking, and I stayed dry by strategically placing my stuff away from the drips. The tips of the hiking poles were completely worn out from the rocks I encountered in New Hampshire. My shorts were ripped but still holding together. My backpack had quite a few rips, however, I was not losing any gear. And my shoes were held in place with duct tape. It was time for my adventure to come to an end.

I was exhausted and in a lot of pain. There were thunderstorms almost every night that kept the rocks and roots wet, which caused me to fall a lot. In Maine there are more roots than any of the other states. I found that the harder it was getting to the top of a mountain, the greater the reward when it came to the amazing scenery. Saddleback Mountain was no exception. The views were breathtaking.

There were a lot of ponds made by beaver dams; however, I had to be extra careful where I would get my water because I did not want to get beaver fever. It was fairly easy to stay somewhat clean since I could get a dip almost every day in a lake or pond. I had never seen so many toads, they were everywhere on the trail. I had to watch every step not to walk on them especially early in the morning. Sometimes they would jump as I was just landing my feet and I did crush a few that I could not avoid.

The AT usually hits every peak possible. For some reason, however, it bypasses Sugarloaf peak in Maine. The trail went around the summit just on the edge. Coming down Sugarloaf was the most threatening and frightening decent I had done yet. It was extremely steep and there were boulders with drops from ten to fifteen feet. Being so close to the finish I was extra careful not to get hurt, but I still manage to fall three times just getting down. I did not get seriously hurt in any of the crashes, but I was still in pain. I had cuts on my left leg, and it was bleeding quite a lot. I was so happy that day that the rocks and roots were dry, otherwise it would have even been a whole lot worse.

On July Fourth the heat became unbearable, but I had already decided to head into Stratton. I ran out of food that morning and came across a SOBO shortly before getting to the trailhead. He gave me a couple of protein cookies. I desperately needed to get some food, so I figured I would take an easy day, especially during the hottest part of the day. Just as I got to the road around eight in the morning, Eagle showed up and decided even though he did not need anything in town he was going to join me to get away from the heat. It was early, but it was already very hot. We hitched into town and got a ride with just the second vehicle going by. It was a woman with a pickup. She said her dog was not friendly, so we had to ride in the back. It was five miles to the nearest store and the wind felt so nice.

The first thing we did in town was get some food. I bought six deviled eggs along with two yogurts and an orange juice. Eagle got a half gallon of ice cream. I scarfed down my food in five minutes and I was still hungry. I am allergic to ice cream, so I was glad to find that this convenient store had frozen yogurt. So I bought a half gallon. I did not expect to eat it all but to my surprise I did not leave a drop. After our good breakfast I bought enough food to get me to Monson.

We were in no hurry to get back on the trail in the extreme heat. Even though cooler weather was coming, they were advising people to stay inside that day. We went to the Laundromat to wash our clothes. Normally there is a washroom where I could change and put on my rain gear when I did laundry, but this one did not have a restroom. We took turns hiding behind the machines to change before we put the load in the washer. While waiting on the machine to do its thing, I noticed that we had just changed under a surveillance camera. After drying our clothes and charging our cell phones, we went to the other side of the road where there was another convenient store. There were a few items I still wanted to get. Once we got there, we found out that they had fried chicken, so we both ate nine pieces of chicken.

Hitching back to the trail was a breeze. Again the second car picked us up. Folks in Maine were extremely friendly and helpful to hikers. It was around three that afternoon when we got back to the trailhead. To our surprise a hiker who had been sent by a nearby hostel, was there giving out ice cream, water, and electrolyte drinks to help out any hiker he saw because of the heat. Eagle ate three more bowls of ice cream before we headed back onto the trail. I had a bunch of cookies. Since the midday sun had passed, we decided we could climb the mountain and make it past South Horn Peak and Bigelow West Peak. There was a campsite just past the west peak. Even though I had not hiked much that day, the climb was considerably hard in the heat. Above the tree line, it got much cooler and when we got to the second peak; it was the most incredible vista I had seen. We had a clear 360-degree view and spent as much time enjoying it as possible. Once we got to the campsite, I went to get some water, but the spring had dried up. I had barely enough water to get me through the night.

Eagle had asked me to wake him up the next morning, so he could get an early start because a bad storm was coming. We were the only people there, and our tents were about fifty yards apart. The next morning it was very windy when I awoke around four. I yelled "EAGLE" a few times from inside my tent to wake him up. Once I climbed out of my tent, I noticed there were two more tents closer to me than Eagle's tent. Those people were probably wondering why on earth somebody would yell eagle at four in the morning. I had to go over to Eagle's tent to wake him up because all the yelling hadn't worked. I told him I would head out first since he was faster than me. We would meet on the trail further down the mountain.

That storm hit us real hard, and the temperature dropped by at least twenty degrees in just a few hours. It went from extreme heat the day before to blistering wind and very cold on top of the mountains. Later that morning I found a patch of blueberries. Most were still white, but

I enjoyed a having few ripe ones. At lunch I waited for about two hours for Eagle, but he never showed up. We were supposed to cross the Kennebec River together the next day. After a while I figured he would catch up with me in the evening. It is dangerous to cross that river by foot in the event that they open the dams up river. The ATC supplies a canoe to assist hikers at the crossing, but you have to show up between 9:30 a.m. and 2:00 p.m. In order to line up to cross the next day I had to set up camp a short distance from the river. I later learned that Eagle was not feeling well that morning; he probably ate too much ice cream the day before. I was hoping he would eventually catch up, but I never saw him again.

I showed up at ten the next morning and was the first NOBO to cross. I had just passed the last hurdle, the last landmark before contacting Lucille to come and get me. I knew I was about thirty-six hours from my final destination in Monson. This was it! Unless I broke a bone, I was going to complete the hike. It was perfect timing because it was a Saturday morning, and I knew she would probably be home and available to come the next day to pick me up. She was expecting my call, but I still had no cell reception. On the north side of the river there is a small town called Caratunk. I stopped at a friendly bed-and-breakfast and asked to use the phone since they had a landline. To my delight Lucille answered the phone, and I was able to arrange for her to come pick me up the next afternoon. It was such a great feeling. After over three months in the wilderness, I was finally going home.

After that phone call sadness set in. I was so happy to finally know that the next day was going to be my last day, but at the same time, I was also extremely sad it was going to be my last night sleeping in my tent. I had grown fond of my tent and got used to my sleeping bag. I felt like a king in my personal castle. I knew the next night I would no longer have the freedom I had enjoyed over the past 107 days. I needed to go home; I wanted to go home, but I did not want to lose the freedom I had been enjoying on the trail. I knew I'd never be able to relive this experience. It had been the most enjoyable thing I had ever done. It had been hard but at the same time it was rewarding. I took an extra-long time that night to pick the perfect spot for my tent and took a long time setting it up. My emotions were running so high once I was in my sleeping bag. It didn't seem that long ago I had set out on Springer Mountain for a journey of a lifetime, but it also felt like an eternity.

The last morning I took my time getting up. I knew I had plenty of time to reach the trailhead where I had arranged for Lucille to pick me up. I had done quite a bit more mileage the day before than I had expected, so I could take it easy. I had to ford two rivers that day, but I knew they would be easy to cross since it had been dry recently. I met a section hiker who was going northbound.

He was complaining about mosquitoes. I offered to give him my deet, but he told me he refused to put on any chemical on his body. He said he had some natural stuff he was going to use in the Hundred-Mile Wilderness coming up after Monson, but he did not have enough so he was waiting till the pests got really bad. I suggested he try it before just in case it did not work because the little beasts can be ferocious in the swampy sections of the Hundred-Mile Wilderness. He assured me it would work even though he had never tried it. I wished him well and offered mine for the last time since it was my last day, but I did not insist.

Moxy Bald was the last summit with no trees and with a 360-degree view I passed. It is not a high mountain; it felt more as a hill after the big peaks I had been going over. As I was climbing my legs got quite week and shaky. I was getting so emotional, and it was making me tremble. I knew this was my last charming panorama. I was emotionally breaking down; I had never felt that way before in my life. I was so sad that I could have easily cried. I tried to hold my emotions even though it did not really matter if I cried since I was alone.

Finally on July 8, I walked out of the woods. It had been eighteen years to the day that I had my last drink of alcohol. I had just accomplished another great achievement. It had been a hard and tough undertaking, fighting the weather, bugs, loneliness, pain, and hunger.

The success of that day was but a fraction of what I achieved eighteen years before. Having to overcome my dependence on alcohol was ten times harder and even more rewarding than walking 2190 miles alone in the Appalachian Mountains.

About the Author

Louis M. Cormier managed to conquer his addiction and turned his life around. He has since, thru-hiked the Appalachian Trail in 2018, backpacked the Huayhuash trek, and did four days of horseback riding in the remote mountains in Peru. He thru-hiked the International Appalachian Trail in New Brunswick, Canada, and Maine, USA. He also hiked the Cape Chignecto and Fundy Footpath (FFP) several times including one trek of the FFP in under twenty-four hours. He is a licensed salmon-fishing guide and loves fly-fishing. Louis has completed over ten marathons, is a four-time Ironman finisher and he has also organised several local races.

Louis has also been sober for over nineteen years. You can reach him at lmcloc@gmail.com.

Made in the USA
Monee, IL
13 May 2020